Our Dementia
A Memoir

Tracy Kauffman Wood

www.auctuspublishers.com

Copyright © 2020 Tracy Kauffman Wood
Book and cover design by Sarah Eldridge
Cover photo and back cover photo by Anthony Wood

Published by Auctus Publishers
606 Merion Avenue, First Floor
Havertown, PA 19083

Printed in the United States of America

Our Dementia: A Memoir is a work of creative non-fiction. The events recounted are to the best of the author's memory. Some names have been altered to protect the privacy of those involved.

All rights reserved. Scanning, uploading, and distribution of this book via the internet or via any other means without permission in writing from its publisher, Auctus Publishers, is illegal and punishable by law. Please purchase only authorized electronic edition.

ISBN 978-1-7334456-3-4 (electronic)
ISBN 978-1-7334456-4-1 (print)

Library of Congress Control Number: 2020943308

Pre-production reviews for
Our Dementia: A Memoir

"Rich in detail, filled with a love of life and anchored in relationships, *Our Dementia* traces the inevitable path of this insidious disease as it affects an entire family. Through the lens of a daughter coming to grips with her mother's illness, we experience the impact of dementia in each of its facets. *Our Dementia* offers insight and support to others who are also travelling on this same difficult road, reminding them that they are not alone."

Cindy Glass Weinraub, Assistant Director of Recreation & Volunteers, Seashore Gardens Living Center

"*Our Dementia* is a loving and spirited memoir written by a daughter who shares her mother's great zest for life, and so cannot imagine the heartache that will come when her mother is struck by a disease that leaves most of us gasping for breath, let alone words. The shared pronoun in the title says everything about what Tracy Kauffman Wood has done—this is a multi-generational memoir focusing on two strong women that honors ancestors, our immigrant past, and the tenacity of those who will not let their family become diminished, despite the ravages of age and time."

Nancy K. Barry, Author of *Lessons from Cancer College*

"A daughter's difficult and very real struggle to help her mother through the end stage of life, dementia and the greater struggle of letting her mother go. Beautifully written and emotionally charged. I have seen these situations happen so many times in my long career and in my personal experience, as I went through the end of life journey with my mother and her dementia. There is so much each of us can learn and take comfort in, as we read Tracy Kauffman Wood's story."

Robin Schneller-Frankwich, M.Ed, N.H.A., Sr., Healthcare Executive in Long Term Care

To humankind—our global family

Foreword

Memoirs can convey a number of narratives: a personal reminiscence about a part of the author's life; recalling interactions with family, friends and others while breathing life into the characters; recounting the author's challenges, failures, successes, traumas, and euphorias; elevating the story from the merely personal to the universal so the reader can identify with at least a portion of the work; and finally, doing so in a writing style that brings the reader into the author's world and with each eagerly turned page, into the story itself.

In *Our Dementia: A Memoir*, Tracy Kauffman Wood has accomplished what most memoirists can only dream of; she has fulfilled all of the possibilities a memoir can achieve. There is the story of a family—the Kravitz clan's progenitors Max and Ida, their ten children born in the first two decades of the 20th century, and their offspring--the author's countless cousins; the milieu in which the author grew up of mostly first and second generation American Jews with family roots embedded in Eastern Europe; the complex relationship of Tracy and her mom culminating in the challenges presented by Sylvia's cognitive decline and the daughter coming to grips with her mom's mortality; navigating the conflicting demands on Tracy by mother, family, and work. In other words, a story all so common in twenty-first century America.

While there is much to which the reader can relate, it's "family"—the very essence of Wood's memoir—that speaks to almost everyone. Wood examines the Kravitz family, both warts and wonders, exploring their humanity and the impact they have on her and one another. There is humor and pathos, jealousy and sacrifice, love and resentment all engagingly written to read like a novel yet meticulously true. In other words, it is about everything that makes a family. Wood writes of a twentieth century Jewish family, but it can easily be Irish, Italian, Chinese, Indian, Hispanic, African, and so on—indeed, almost anyone's family.

And within the author's immediate family, firmly fixed in the center like a ship's anchor holding the vessel in place and from drifting off course, is the matriarch. Sylvia is Tracy's mother, but she can just as well be anyone's mother, and Tracy is Sylvia's daughter, but she can be just about be anyone's daughter. At its heart, this is the story of Sylvia and Tracy when that anchor becomes unmoored. It is a story of a parent and a child when the child reluctantly becomes the parent. What can be more universal than that?

Richard D. Bank, author of *I Am Terezin* and *Feig*

Preface

My grandparents, Ida and Max Kravitz had ten children—Joe, Herman, Eva, Jean, Lena, Bess, Minnie, Jack, Sylvia and Lenny. Niece Lillian, (Joe's daughter) was raised by my grandparents as well. When speaking about a sister or brother, the Kravitz siblings referred to each other as "Our Bess" or "Our Sylvie". Being born, or marrying into the clan gave you the status of being ours, or someone else's within the family. When the older siblings took spouses, whose names duplicated that of a sibling, possessive forms naturally followed, such as "Herman's Lena" and "Jack's Lil". It was all so ingrained in the family lexicon that as a grandchild, I assumed that Jack's was Lil's first name. I believe that this possessive our-ness evolved in response to their impoverished, immigrant childhood. It allowed them to have something to share with the world. And what they had was each other and their stories. Bubbe Ida always said, "We may not have money, but we're rich in family."

The reference of our was visited on the next generation. For example, I remember my mother saying to her friends, "Our Tracy got her Master's," or "Our Tracy bought a house." (Although, she only used it to begin a narrative about me of which she was proud. She would never say, "Our Tracy got suspended from school." That she would not own.) Our-ness became more precious and poignant to the siblings as they began losing each other. For example, when Aunt Bess died, I remember my mother's stark message on my answering machine, "Our Bess is gone." Collective loss as well as collective ownership was heightened by the use of our.

Being "Our Tracy" gave me an origin in the world—a place from which to start, and a place to feel secure enough to leave. And as I watched my mother's siblings pass away, while Mom was left alone to endure the indignity of losing her mind, my original place in this community of our-ness summoned me home. I owed it to her parents and siblings. I must save "Our Sylvie". She might be losing her status in the world, but never in our family. It was beyond responsibility or duty. It was the power of our-ness, unaffected by death. It felt visceral, like an electrical charge through my being connecting to the closed circuit of our family. I was charged by my mother's deceased siblings to assist her through slow death. Not one of them had experienced death in this way and not one of her siblings remained to see her through it. I knew that her sisters would have been beside her, because our-ness was cultivated in them since childhood. It was a potential, a hidden light switch in a closet we all inherited. I was called to flip this switch and cast our family's light—a hidden reserve, on this dark and lonely day.

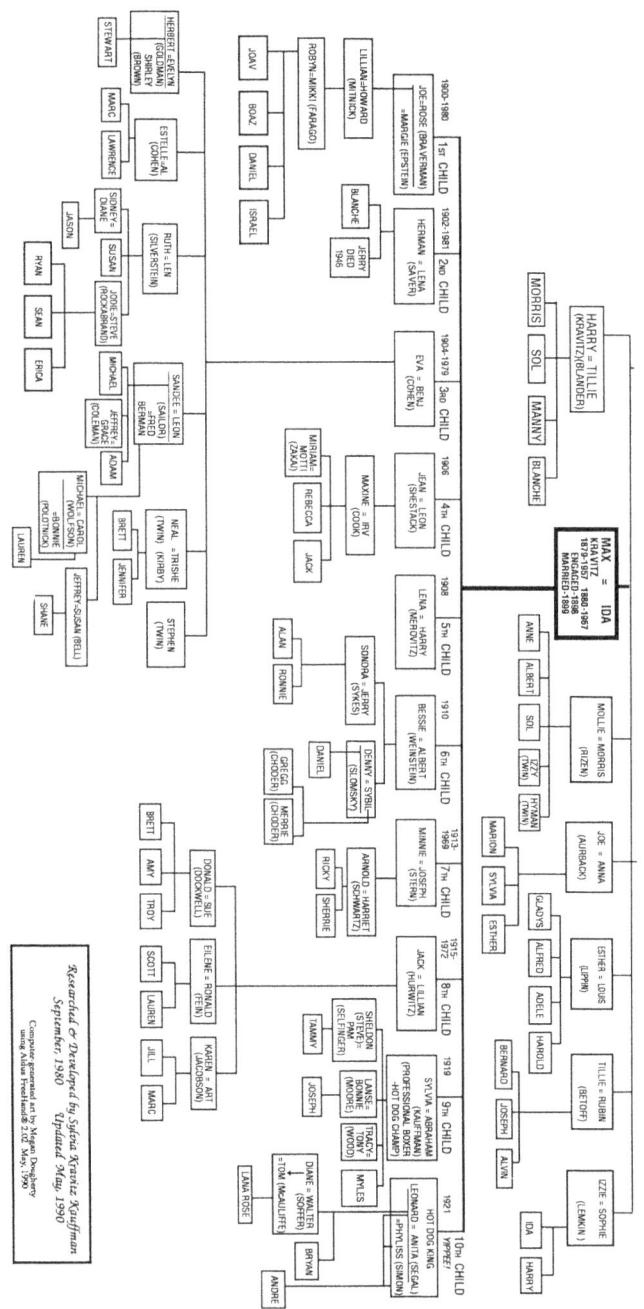

Friday Night at Bubbe's

Summer, 1967

Every Friday night, Bubbe Ida's dining room table becomes her canvas, stretching centuries, laden with chicken soup, matzo balls, boiled chicken, kugel, challah, bowties and kasha, and of course, her own k'mish bread. Our family, as well as any other neighbors or friends who pick up on the aroma, crowd into her four-room row house apartment at 6727 Horrocks Street, Northeast Philadelphia, to eat in shifts.

Those coming directly from work, along with the children, are fed first. The second shift pokes around the living room looking at the same old photographs, munching on salted peanuts and chocolate kisses, smoking or just squeezing together on the sofa, gulping down the rich, luscious air of Bubbe's house.

Aunt Jean, just home from work, still wearing her Lenny's Hot Dogs uniform, dutifully sits in the same chair each week while Bubbe brings her soup. Aunt Jean serves fast food at a hot dog stand at Fifth and Passyunk Avenue all day to people she calls "baby" and "doll." She willingly surrenders her public persona as Bubba's steamy soup seeps through her. She ends her meal with a Raleigh cigarette. She lets me count the coupons. She chews Dentyne and carries four packs in her handbag, always one there for me.

Aunt Min and Aunt Bess hover around the table, broad jumping to the refrigerator, should any man or child ask for ketchup or butter. Bubbe can't understand why anyone needs ketchup so you won't find any on the table, and butter is "tref," not kosher with chicken. It isn't allowed. But no one knows from want at Bubbe's house, so with impish delight Aunt Minnie and Aunt Bessie make sure that the contraband gets into the right hands.

No one waits very long for anything. In fact, the second shift usually ends up at the table with the slower eaters of the first shift, who are unwilling and often unable to give up their thrones. The table talk usually centers around the hot dog business. Almost everyone works for Uncle Lenny except for my parents, who have their own luncheonette, Abie's Hot Dogs at Fourth and Monroe. Aunt Bess works at Lenny's on Castor Avenue. Aunt Minnie does not, although her husband, Uncle Joe started working for Lenny after he lost his last job.

The sisters Min and Bess resemble each other sharing many of the same facial features and a similar sense of humor. Aunt Bessie is a brunette. Aunt Minnie dyes her hair fire-engine-red. People often see Bess working the counter at Lenny's on Castor and remark, "Oh, you've darkened your hair!"

"No, you're thinking of my sister, our Minnie," she replies. The words "my sister, our Minnie" drip from her mouth sweet as pie-a-la-mode, famishing any sister-less soul like me.

Cousin Lily is one of the oldest grandchildren, only a few years younger than my mother, Sylvia, and her younger brother, Lenny. When Lily's mother died young, Bubbe Ida took in Lily. She was the last of the eleven children that Bubbe raised. Lily doesn't work for Lenny and is proud of it. She wears bright, tight clothes over her ample frame and every inch of her says "Notice me!!" I imagine this is to be expected from the eleventh child. She complains that the cigarette smoke on Friday night at Bubbe's irritates her asthma, and that there is "too much food". She doesn't stay long, but like all of Bubbe's children, she always finishes her plate. My own Auntie Mame, Cousin Lily drives a convertible and takes me away on weekends to Long Beach Island, New Hope, movies, and the theater. She whets my appetite for the freedom and excitement of the road, as well as the comfortable embrace of returning home.

This is the table where I spend every Friday night. I am one of the kids that Bubbe Ida feeds first. I watch the quiver of her wrinkled, vein striped hands as she carries my bowl of hot soup between them. She doesn't flinch when that steamy broth leaks down her sagging arms towards her elbows. Bubbe crossed an ocean to bring me that soup. Feeding me is her goal. Mortal affliction will not come between us. The soup contains her hopes for a better life for herself, her family, and her world. It makes the struggles of her past, as well as the creeping injustices of old age recede into the background, at least on Friday night. Bubbe infuses her children, my cousins, my brothers, and me with her fire, and fortifies us with the soup that is her antidote to physical or spiritual suffering. She encourages us to feed the fire of life and to dignify its dying embers. Soon, she will leave 25 grandchildren who will, in turn, have grandchildren of their own.

Come to the Cemetery with Me

Fall, 1997

"How 'bout it, Trace? Come to the cemetery with me," Mom asks. "I go every year in the fall before the Jewish holidays. I'd like you to see what I do. How about joining me next Wednesday?"

"If you take me to lunch afterwards I'll go," I reply, knowing full well that is part of the deal. I'm flippant and not too excited about this outing with Mom. I feel like I'm doing her a favor by accompanying her. She can tell. I'm 41 years old but Mom brings out the stubborn teenager in me. Even though I look forward to my days off with her, even though I find the cemetery to be somewhat interesting, even though I affectionately remember our deceased family members; somehow if she suggests it and there seems to be a lesson involved about growing up and taking responsibility, then I am compelled to show resistance.

"There's a great diner nearby that serves breakfast all day. Daddy and I used to go there after the cemetery for western omelet sandwiches." She baits me.

"Okay. We're on," I say. The promise of my favorite diner breakfast—sunny-side-up eggs dripping over hash browns and buttered toast—makes the rest of the trip more palatable for me, leaving much less room to object.

Mom drives to my house the following Wednesday morning. I greet her in the driveway and she hands me her car keys. "How about driving my car? I'd like you to know how to get there."

Her oversized key ring is more like a bracelet, allowing her to find her keys wherever she has last left them. I rotate and rattle the ring around my wrist as if it were a hula-hoop. Why do I need to know how to get there? Does she want me to carry on this tradition without her? Is that what she's saying? I don't want to think about a time without her. I want to think that this time in our lives will go on forever. She doesn't push these concerns on me; she just slips them in every once in a while. Maybe that's what bothers me, the indirectness of it. But when she tries to be direct with me about her own mortality, I push it aside saying, "We don't need to talk about that now." After all, she is just as vibrant and enthusiastic as always, whether we are going to the cemetery or the theater. Her body is in great shape. She takes exercise and dance classes, swims and walks the track at her gym. Her face is open and engaging as ever, although her years can now be counted in its wrinkles.

"Don't get too close!" she demands when my husband Tony and I approach her with our ever-present cameras. She is hypersensitive about the lines in her face as if they exist to betray her, showing the age she would just as soon deny. She still colors her hair reddish blond and blow-dries it herself for a youthful, casual look. She swims three days a week, so why bother with a hair salon? Her bright, hazel eyes rarely show fatigue as she drives herself from one activity to the next. I take way more naps than she does.

When I was a kid I thought that my mother was too happy. I remember Mom bragging to a friend's mother, "I'm going to the opera tonight, root, toot, toot!"

"Root, toot, too-oot?" Mom's enthusiasm for life embarrassed me. Of course, she was genuinely thrilled to leave behind the demands of children, an aging mother, and my father's thankless luncheonette business to indulge in a night at the opera. It's not that Mom wasn't grateful for my father's devotion to earning a living for us. It's just that the constant burglaries and meager income hardly seemed worth the hundred hours per week he often clocked.

Joie de vivre was something Mom consciously passed on to my three brothers and me when she took us to the theatre on school nights, impressing upon us the importance of culture and celebration over sleep. "You'll sleep when you die!" she'd boldly pronounce, shrugging off sleep with a wave of her hand, and shuttling us from a rousing evening at the

Academy of Music to cap off the night with pie-a-la-mode at the Melrose Diner. I remember spotting Mrs. Seltzer, my first-grade teacher in the lobby during the intermission of "La Boheme" at the Academy. I was six years old and it was 8:30 p.m. on a Tuesday night.

"Hey look! There's Mrs. Seltzer." I said to Mom.

"Go say hello," Mom said. "Show her how much culture ya got!"

I skipped across the lobby, flushed with my mother's pride in my maturity and depth. "Hi Mrs. Seltzer. It's me, Tracy. I'm here at the opera with my mom."

"You ought to be home in bed!" She scolded. Tears welled up in my eyes as I returned to my mother. I was learning that not everybody thought like Mom.

After Mom's mother, Bubbe Ida died, and my youngest brother, Myles started school, Mom took an office job with the federal government. This took her away from the stress of the luncheonette, allowed her children more independence, and gave her the benefits that my father's small business never could. She retired after 25 years of government work just four years ago, around the time of my father's death. Now she enjoys her pension, her boyfriend, and her classes at the senior center. She has taken the "Sleep when you die" maxim into retirement with her. She keeps busy.

It's warm in the sun, but a slight undercurrent of fresher, cooler air brushes my shoulders as we prepare to leave. Although it's late September just before the High Holidays, we're still wearing the sleeveless shirts of summer. It's traditional to visit the cemetery at the beginning of the Jewish New Year, to say a prayer at the stones of deceased loved ones and perhaps ask for intercession. I remember Mom's trips to the cemetery when I was a child, especially after Bubbe died. I never went. I wonder why she asks me to go with her now and not my brothers. Of course, my eldest brother Steve lives in California, but both Lanse and Myles live within a couple hours from her and visit often. My house happens to be conveniently located between hers and the cemetery. But I know it's more than that.

"Take a light jacket. I always do," Mom suggests.

I go back into the house to grab a ragged sweatshirt. Again, I'm feeling put upon but I do what she says. It's the sweatshirt I wear in the darkroom when developing film. It's stained from fixer but it separates me from her. I'm not just her daughter, doing her daughterly duty; I'm a busy photographer who is gracing Mom with her valuable time. I am constantly creating this distance between us. She puts up with it. Years ago, she abandoned her suggestions on how to dress or wear my hair. Mom dresses up for our outing, and for me. She accessorizes her multi-color, polyester pantsuit by wearing orange lipstick and a costume jeweled necklace with matching clip-on earrings. Her outfit is unstained, and suggests her joy in spending a little time with me.

"Just follow Route One South," Mom instructs, as I back out of the driveway, tires squealing. "Mt. Sharon Cemetery is where a lot of our family is buried. Maybe you'll visit them when I'm gone."

Mom and I laugh at this unlikely scenario, even as she suggests it. Neither of us is sure which is more unlikely–that she will ever die, or that I will visit the cemetery, if and when she does. We never talk about what will happen after she's gone, except in jest. She is so alive and vibrant, more so than people half her age. I can't imagine her any other way, or what I'll do when she's not around. So, I don't. She never demands or tells me what she wants outright. Instead she says, "How about it, Trace?" But she has just turned 78 and I'm realizing that this is more than just another mother/daughter outing. Mom wants to share her ritual with me, so that I might continue it.

As usual, I distance my heart from my mother's reach. At 41, I'm still borrowing my responses from the past. Perhaps I think it will keep us both young. I never encourage her to downsize or to have me check in on her finances. I see no further than her smile.

Despite my flippancy, I love being with my mother. She values everything I say. She makes me feel important. She speaks to the best of me and seems content to ignore the rest. When she says, "Y' know Trace..." my heart instinctively smiles in her direction, before my mind does an edit. ("This is just my mother. I don't need to be nice to her. She'll love me anyway.") The salve of her voice allows past, present and future to meld, when I allow myself to relax into it. She soothes my vulnerability. Worry dissolves. I'm a child again and she indulges the worst of my childish habits. We each half-try to stop each other. But why should we stop? We're comfortable with the pattern.

I turn into the stone-pillared entrance of Mt. Sharon Cemetery. I relax as we pass row after row of boxy monuments. I'm struck by its uncanny resemblance to the Northeast Philadelphia neighborhood in which I was raised, and where my mother still lives, with its ordered rows of upright, vertical homes, each with its own measured and manicured square of grass in front. Familiar with this venue, my mother quickly guides me toward her parents' stones. I park the car by the side of the road.

"Wear good shoes for walking when you come here, Sweetheart." The lesson continues. When will she realize that I always wear sneakers? The ground is uneven and the graveled road on which we walk needs paving.

Mom and I are the same height. She has lost a couple of inches with age and I never made it quite past five feet. When we walk side-by-side, she takes three short, quick steps to my one long stride. We keep up with each other, but pace ourselves differently. As long as I've known her, she has walked like someone with much to do and little time; whereas I leisurely stroll through life without much direction and all the time in the world.

We approach the side-by-side stones that read, "Kravitz—Max and Ida." Max's dates are noted as 1879-1957. Ida's are 1880-1967. Mom turns away from me, leans against their stones and speaks in Yiddish to her parents while I watch. Mom is slumped over, not standing erect as usual. She seems to close in on herself with her shoulders forward, protecting her heart. She speaks softly, almost to herself. Her voice becomes brittle, like a child's. It's quiet around us and the lawn has been freshly mowed. It smells like Sundays in the summers of my childhood, when Dad mowed the lawn and listened to the ballgame. I breathe, relax, and listen.

"Mom, Pop, mear zite Tzivelle, Ich hub dear lieb. Alla mul du bist in mina heartz. Di gantse velt iz sheyn." With these strange yet familiar sounds, Mom gently taps at the fragile shell of distance between worlds. She is animated and respectful as she speaks to her immigrant parents, like an eight-year-old just home from a class trip, reporting on the wonder of the day's events.

I feel as if I'm watching my mother as a child in her parents' living room—one that I've never seen. Except, she's play-acting a bit for my benefit. She steals a glance at me, in the midst of her dialogue, to see if I'm watching. Finally, she stands upright, turns, and looks at me with a smile.

"What did you just say?" I ask.

"Umm, I just said Mom, Pop, It's me, your Sylvie. I love you. All the time you are in my heart. The whole world is beautiful."

She seems surprised at how it sounds aloud, in English. We both fight tears. We walk about fifty feet across to her sister-in-law Rose's grave. The façade of the stone is shattered and broken. It leans sideways from the enormous tree roots beneath it, burrowing through its faded face. But it can still be read. It says, "Rose Kravitz, Died August 6, 1926, Aged 26 years." This grave is older than any of those surrounding. "This is your cousin Lily's mother. Rose was my eldest brother Joe's first wife. She died when Lily was three. I was seven. Then, niece Lily came to live with us. My mother raised her. Mom would bring our Lily here to visit this stone every year until she was grown. She didn't want Lily to forget her mother."

I imagine my grandmother standing at Rose's unscathed and upright grave. A small child leans on the young tree beside them, with none of these other stones around. My mother doesn't remember Rose. But she remembers Lily complaining about the long, boring trolley ride from their home in South Philadelphia to this cemetery, in what used to be the country and is now an aging suburb, just to stare at a stone. Mom recalls Lily's angry, grief-tainted recriminations to Bubbe, her grandmother, "But it's not my mother. It's just a stone!"

A year after this September outing with Mom, we will be back with garden tools, burying Lily's ashes in the open crevices created by the tree's expanding roots. Lily will die after a short illness in September of 1998. At the age of 75, she will leave one daughter and four grandsons. She will be cremated. Her daughter Robyn, who lives abroad, will wish neither to fly her mother's ashes home with her, nor to burden someone else with them. Shortly after Lily's memorial service, Mom and I will accompany Robyn to the cemetery, where Mom will be the lookout as it is illegal to tamper with established monuments, while Robyn and I deepen the holes surrounding Rose's stone. My fingers will dig through the cold, muddy soil. I'll push it aside in mounds, like dark sand castles. We'll pour Lily's ashes into our carved-out spaces between roots, quickly patch them with clumps of wet dirt, and gently smooth the top with a small shovel. We'll say a quick prayer for Lily, feeling sure that this is where she would want to be–finally at rest with her mother.

And while we're here, we'll have other ashes to bury. My mother's youngest brother Lenny's remains will also accompany us. Lenny will die five weeks before Lily. After his memorial service, Lenny's widow will give his ashes to my mother. While we're here, we'll find yet another solution to the problem of accumulating family remains. We'll stop at Max and Ida's graves. Remarkably, there will be a deep hole beneath the stone. This is where we will pour Lenny's ashes, patting them down with mud. "Perfect," my mother will say. "Back to his mother—who loved him most of all."

Then we'll get the hell out of there, before we get arrested. On the way home, we'll boast of our two-for-one burial bargain, not to mention the avoidance of over seventy years of inflation. Mom will recall a story from her childhood as the older sister and aunt to Lenny and Lily, respectively.

"Bubbe said to me, 'Tzivelle, here's a quarter. Take the kids to the grocer's for lunch today. I'll be working. Then go directly back to school.' Bubbe Ida gave me a quarter to buy lunch for myself, eight-year-old Lenny, and six-year-old Lily. At ten years old, I was proud to be entrusted with this responsibility."

Mom will sit up straight in the car and throw her shoulders back.

"Choosing our lunch was my decision alone to make. That quarter made me feel powerful. I flipped it in my sweating palm all morning as I sat at my desk in school, waiting for the noon buzzer to ring. Then I gathered Lenny and Lily from their classrooms and headed off to the grocery store at Fourth and South. I knew what I wanted and where to find it, but still I considered my options as I perused the two, over-stocked aisles of Pop's Grocery. Finally, with my heart set and that quarter burning a hole in my pocket, I reached for the Tastykake Chocolate Cupcakes wrapped in a cellophane package of three. Just perfect for the three of us, I thought. Just the sound of the cellophane beneath my fingers made me salivate. I tried hard not to mess up the smooth icing as I lay them on the counter. I thought, it's perfect—one cupcake per kid for Lenny, Lily and me. Then I saw the Pepsi and I knew we had to have it. That bubbling bottle of soda would be just enough for each of us to wash down a cupcake. We never got that at home, and the total cost for both purchases—just twenty-five cents! I'm sure I was beaming at the grocer. He must've realized how smart I was. He let me snap off the bottle cap at the metal bottle opener attached to the wall behind the counter. I inhaled the smoke from the fizz as the cap dropped. Ahhhh! That sensation was pleasure enough—but soon, because of my choice, we'd all be sipping a rare treat. Lenny and Lily were digging through the bottle caps in the bucket below. I felt great when our bottle cap fell into their waiting hands. I settled them down on the Fourth Street sidewalk outside the store, and doled out the cupcakes. We took our time. A sip of Pepsi for each of us after every bite. I made sure that no one guzzled it down. This was not a lunch we'd get at home. At home, there would be a little soup and maybe some mashed potatoes with chicken fat— schmaltz, Bubbe called it. We would finish our plates, as was expected. But on the sidewalk, we giggled as we ate and serenaded each other— braap!—with healthy belches. 'Leave it to us kids to know what's good!' we all repeated, punctuated with a burp. Then Lenny returned the empty bottle to its compartment on the wooden Pepsi tray inside the store. The grocer gave him a penny. I watched Lenny shove it into his pants pocket, unannounced. But I didn't say anything. We went back to school for the afternoon. 'Tzivelle?' Bubbe asked me later that evening. 'How'd you make out with the quarter for lunch?'

'Mom, we had Tastykake Chocolate Cupcakes. The package held three, just right for three kids—one for each of us and a bottle of Pepsi we shared to wash it down. It was great!'

Bubbe replied, 'Very good, but you could've bought milekh' That second syllable, which Bubbe added to the word 'milk' from the Yiddish 'milekh,' was higher pitched than the first. It dangled like a question. That dangling syllable left me hanging, questioning my perfect choice. It left a disappointingly guilty aftertaste to my independent triumph— an aftertaste so strong, I'm remembering it today. Certainly, I could buy milk next time for my siblings, and dutifully I did. But when it came to my life and my kids, there would be milk and Pepsi. Unlike Bubbe, I came of age in a world of choice and opportunity. I had the luxury to admit that although milk may be healthier, there are times when nothing beats a Pepsi! Like right now. Come on, let's go get some!"

And so, we will. While Robyn, Mom, and I each sip from our own bottle of Pepsi, it will occur to me that we have just fulfilled the last of Mom's responsibilities toward her younger siblings. Of her large nuclear family of thirteen, she and her older sister Lena are the only ones left.

But it is still a year before Lily's and Lenny's death, and we have no idea how we will soon be fortifying the land beneath these family stones. Mom and I continue our ancestral tour.

We walk to a plot of newer monuments, most of them with final dates in the 1970s, '80s and early '90s. It looks like a higher-priced neighborhood, with stones that are less blemished, more intact, and better cared for. It is autumn but the leaves have not yet turned or fallen. Nothing crunches beneath our feet. Our sneakers track the soft, wet earth from one gravestone to the next. I become conscious not to leave a mess. I realize that I've become more emotionally engaged as I witness these relationships coming to life in stories.

We stand at Uncle Ben's stone. Uncle Ben was the husband of my mother's eldest sister, Eva. Uncle Ben's family lived next door to Mom's family on Ellsworth Street in South Philadelphia. Aunt Eva married the boy next door. Uncle Ben had olive-toned skin and crinkly, dark eyes that were always smiling.

"Benny!!!" Mom yells and I jump, half expecting to see him. But no, she's just fussing over his stone, picking at weeds, and brushing away the dirt. It's as if he's about to take her to dinner, so she's fixing his hair and straightening his tie. "Let's go!" she says. I'm not sure if she's talking to him or me.

Mom's sister Bess's grave is next. "MMWWPPAA!" Mom smooches long and loud. "I'm kissing you through the air, Bessele!" Mom's volume rises as she conjures decades of sisterly warmth still thriving. She blows love bubbles into the universe while I watch.

Aunt Bess was as effusive and fun loving as my mother with the same broad build and wide smile, but she was older and more practical. It must've been wonderful for Mom to have a sister like Bess. Bess took care of the family. She baked and sewed. She could fix a vacuum cleaner, a toilet, or a ticket. Bess did what had to be done, allowing Mom to be more self-centered. Mom played tennis and learned to swim. Mom, the youngest of six sisters, was the only one to graduate from high school and continue her education. They were children of immigrants. Bess was the sixth child, the first of Mom's nine siblings to be born in America, at home in a tenement slum. Once when I had asked Bess about her life, she recalled her first memory—watching her mother give birth at home to her brother Jack, when she was five.

"Did your mother's cries scare you?" I had asked her.

"No," Bessie responded. "I knew she was having a baby and the pain was worth it."

Bessie matured with clear and simple values. Work hard, keep your house clean, protect, and enjoy your family. That's what counts. The family called Bess, "Betty Frank." She was honest to the point of embarrassment. But it never embarrassed her. She left that job to her older sister Lena.

Aunt Bess's frankness continues to amuse me as I stand at her stone thinking about a luncheon I attended with her back in 1988, along with my aunts Jean and Lena, Mom, Dad, and my husband Tony. We all had been invited to lunch at Tony's parents' home. Emily and Hottea's house was a picture of upper class, 1980s' prosperity with an "old money" sense of style. They lived among the antique trappings of their history. The dining room table was set with linen napkins and a matching tablecloth, with exquisitely carved Chippendale chairs surrounding. Bess was quite impressed with the ceramic name cards at each of our place settings—each name written in erasable pen. "How welcoming, classy and practical!" After a delicious lunch in the formal dining room, Aunt Bess asked to be excused. I escorted her to the powder room located on the lower level. We passed through Emily's "Avalon Room," decorated with a sense of fun and escape like a room at the seashore. In contrast to the heavier, darker furniture on the upper floor, here was a collection of antique dolls and strollers on display and other expensive and frivolous knickknacks from their travels.

"Chatchkes!" Bessie erupted. The waste of space and extra junk annoyed her. "Too much to keep clean! A Jewish person would throw it all out!" she loudly confided to me.

Bess had little time for art and was more impressed by craft. But Bessie's criticisms of others never bothered me. She just called things as she saw them. Thankfully, Bess never mentioned the chatchkes upon our return upstairs. That would have mortified Aunt Lena.

Mom is off to the next gravestone—Cousin Estelle's. A dark beauty, she succumbed to suicide at age 50. "Too much life," I'd heard it said. Estelle had been my mother's childhood friend and niece, (the daughter of Uncle Ben and Aunt Eva). Cousin Estelle inherited Uncle Ben's crinkly, smiling eyes, but when she looked out from old photographs she seemed to be looking toward an even better party. She was not much younger than my mother, and she left two sons, older than me. In silence, I stand next to my mom, remembering Cousin Estelle.

I think back to the last time I saw Estelle, but I don't share this with Mom. We were in Miami together in 1977. Estelle was trying to connect with me, in her way. Chain-smoking and seemingly out of place in the world, she always wanted to find "cool" and live there. As a young married woman, she'd moved from South Philadelphia to Southern California with her new husband. They tuned into drugs, alcohol, and sexual swinging in the late 1950s and early '60s, long before the rest of us turned on. Apparently, that had taken its toll, and was just the beginning of her problems, according to family stories I'd heard. By the time I saw her in 1977, while I briefly visited with Aunt Lena and Uncle Harry in Delray

Beach, she was unable to focus on anything for very long—especially not the movie, *Got, Mentsch, un Taybl, (God, Man and Devil)* playing at the Yiddish Theatre, a stop on Lena and Harry's stock tour of Miami Beach. I was 21, fresh out of college, surveying the country for a lifestyle. At that time, Estelle was 50, and suffering. She was burnt out from indulgence and impatient with abstinence. She was tired of not listening and sick of listening too hard. She was overwrought from making poor decisions, uncomfortable with the decisions others made for her, and empty from either denying her heart or spreading it around too thin.

Estelle pleaded with me, "Let's go to the lobby. Want a cigarette?"

"I don't smoke," I felt bad saying. I didn't tell her I got headaches from other people's smoke.

On that day, twenty years ago, Aunt Lena and Uncle Harry lost patience with niece Estelle's nervous, sloppy, defeated demeanor. Harry and Lena were the opposite of cool, despised anything less than status quo, adored the mainstream, and worshipped the wealthy. Lena was embarrassed by family weakness. Any kind of poverty, material or spiritual, shamed her. Lena and Harry had made a pact early in their marriage of minds: hard work, no exceptions, and no excuses. They defined compassion in dollars. This was Lena's rationale to nurse her heart. After Harry died a decade later, Lena's heart expanded and burrowed through the crust of that loveless marriage. She laughed more easily. But on that day, back in 1977, Lena and Harry gave Cousin Estelle twenty bucks and dropped her off on a Miami sidewalk somewhere. The rest of us were treated to dinner. I didn't say anything to confront them or try to protect Estelle. I just watched and went out to eat, finished my plate to please Aunt Lena, and left feeling empty.

A few months after that day, I was camping on a beach in California when I heard that Estelle's body had washed up on Miami Beach alone. Estelle—a burst bubble, a dead jellyfish no one wanted to touch. Her two sons on another coast had tried. Her parents tried, in their way. They'd brought her to Miami. Her sadness was their burden. They were all shadows of their former selves, too much heartache untreated.

My mother stands in silence for a moment in front of Estelle's stone. I sense Mom's need to make this a positive experience for me. She wants me to remember Estelle the way she does. Mom's effervescence erupts into the silence surrounding us. Each syllable propels the next. Pow! Pow! Pow!

"Stel, your kids are doing great BABY!!"

It is less like an exploding Pepsi and more like an Atlantic City ocean wave carrying all of us to shore. I smell the Noxzema, taste salt, chew sand, and search for loud-colored Florida towels featuring buxom gals in scant bikinis— towels smelling like Tide, spread and flattened by the fat, familiar bodies of my aunts and cousins of ample bosom in ruffled, one-piece, skirted bathing suits, dipping pretzels into mustard.

My mother's enthusiasm is a dab of healing salve anointing the past, present, and future. She chooses Pepsi when milk might be more sensible. Her zest for life refreshes our family, living and dead. She coats our souls with her whole, beautiful world.

At the diner, afterwards, Mom happily munches on her favorite sandwich—the perfect combination of ham, peppers, eggs and melted cheese squeezed between the toasted white bread of my youth. "Oh, how Daddy and I used to love these western sandwiches." The fact that the ham would lack the approval of their orthodox Jewish parents (however long dead) had made it even more enjoyable for my parents to indulge a guilty pleasure. This was their version of sneaking a joint, I guess.

"I'm glad Dad is buried at a closer cemetery. We thought it would be easier for you kids. This place is so far. There are plenty of good restaurants around there, since it's right by Neshaminy Mall. And of course, I'll be buried next to him. Did I tell you that I'm having a stone bench placed alongside our monuments, engraved 'Kauffman.' So, you'll always have a place to sit and cry."

    Mom loves this new graveside option. She's sure it will come in handy. Meanwhile, I dig my whole-wheat toast into eggs splattered over hash-brown potatoes, washing it down with a Pepsi

The Beginning of the End

Late Fall, 2001

"Trace, I want you to take a look at my books. You need to know where everything is and what to do in case something happens to me. I want you to take charge," Mom says.

"No, no, nothing's going to happen," I insist. "You're fine. No need to do that now." This conversation repeats itself for years over Sunday brunch at Mom's house. Whenever I have arrived a little early or stayed a little later, Mom has pointed me toward her 1950s-era mahogany china closet and I have set the table or returned the dishes to their place behind its regal glass doors.

"That china was an engagement present and they're still showing the Franciscan pattern at Boscov's. I bought you some recently to finish the set. It's stored in the basement. You'll take the china when I'm gone."

For years, Mom has told me this and for years I have ignored the subtext—she is steering me towards the opaque cabinet doors below the china compartment. Mom stores her over-extended, accordion file, jam-packed with receipts and bank statements behind the bottom doors. Now, there is urgency to her tone. She wants me to force open the bottom doors, which tend to stick, and to lay these statements out on the table to admire and scrutinize, as if they were hand-decorated china.

"Trace, you're going to need to know these things." Mom speaks in a hushed tone about "these things" she wants to share. She is a retired bookkeeper and it would please her to turn over the books to me. But I find it boring and irrelevant. I detect that my reluctance to "take over" is a growing concern of hers. But as usual, I ignore her concerns and she doesn't push them on me.

In retirement, she takes charge of her mind/body balance. She swims three days a week, walks the track at her gym, enjoys country western dancing, attends yoga and Tai Chi classes, and sings in a choir. She has season tickets to the theater and orchestra. She has a boyfriend and a bustling social life. Mementos from her travels, photos of her family, and anything else she comes across that pleases her hang from yellowed tape to the mahogany paneled walls of her dining room. Her home is lively and welcoming long after her kids are gone. It smells like the Hershey Kisses overflowing from ashtrays. There is plenty of ice cream in the freezer. Neighborhood children linger. But she lives for Sundays when she plays host to her own children and theirs, any extended family, old friends who are still around, and perhaps a surprise cousin visiting from out of town. Her house is the place where a wandering niece or nephew travels out of their way to visit. Whether they grew up beside her or only met a few times, she made an impression. For my cousins, Aunt Sylvie's house is the highly anticipated and fondly remembered stop along the way.

Sunday after Sunday, year after year, we allow the aroma of coffee, smoked fish, freshly-sliced red onions, and bagels to suspend us in time as we lounge on the sofa reading the paper. She loves carrying on this ritual that had been hers and my father's as far back as I can remember. After Dad's death, she feels it even more important to keep us coming. This is how she welcomes our adopted infant daughter Amity, when Tony and I bring her home from Vietnam in the spring of 1998. Amity delights in speed crawling from wall-to-wall on the thick carpeting and bouncing from one lap to the next. But the lap where she lands is Mom's. When they share their first cone of Breyers vanilla ice cream, their familial bond is cemented.

When Amity turns four, Tony and I treat both my 81-year-old mother and our daughter to Disney World. Mom's favorite ride is "It's A Small World." Amity, on my right, wide-eyed and pointing, hums to the familiar music. Mom, on my left, applauds wildly, yelling "Bravo! Bravo!" as every turn of our craft exposes us to a new scenario of international culture, color, and a cacophony of sound. I squeeze between them, content to be in my own small, perfect world. Afternoons offer Mom and me a chance to relax together. Tony returns to the hotel to nap. Amity falls asleep in the stroller and we find a shaded bench, ice cream cones, and a vantage point from which to view the endless parade of overheated, overspending, T-shirted tourists suspending everyday life to run from one long line to the next at Disney World. We sink into repose.

Who could predict the meteor destined to hit my perfectly crafted world? There is no indication that by the end of the year, I will be sandwiched between my mother and daughter again, with one hand guiding the stroller and the other, the walker. That over the next few years, I will be that determined woman you see in the supermarket pushing forward on my mother's wheelchair while pulling my daughter in the shopping cart behind. Was there a card reader at Disney World who could have foreseen my valiant, futile attempts to rendezvous with the small, perfect world of months before? Finally, in mid-life, I will learn that having a mother doesn't entitle you to remain a child. In fact, as my mother used to say, "The tables will turn." And when they do, there is no turning back.

Mom's world begins to fissure in small ways: senseless arguments with her boyfriend, excessive worry, bouts of crying. Her face takes on a look of sudden fear and indecision. Her brow furrows, her eyes pop and look around in self-defense, her mouth snaps shut in a straight line. Having to choose anything leads to an anxiety attack. "What am I gonna do? What am I gonna do...?" she repeats over and over, second-guessing every decision. She begins depending on stock phrases like "a horse of a different color" to explain how distant she feels from the rest of the world and from herself. When asked by the doctor, or her friends, "Sylvia, how do you feel?" She responds, "I'm in a class by myself."

Often her eyes are vacant. She can get lost and desperate in a house full of people. In fact, one night when a few out-of-town nieces and nephews are in and stop by to visit their Aunt Sylvie, I find her alone and sobbing at the kitchen table, "We have no ice cream, Trace. I can't give them ice cream. The cupboard's bare."

After ten years of near-perfect attendance, she stops walking to the senior center in the mornings. She can't separate from recurring nightmares upon awakening. I begin receiving phone calls from her at 6:00 a.m. "I can't stand it! It's terrible! I want to die! I want to die! Tracy, I know what's coming!" She screams and sobs. "I want to die! The worst is yet to come!" I spend hours on the phone talking her down while trembling in disbelief that this is my energetic, optimistic, happy-go-lucky mother.

"Go out!" I say. "Go dancing, walk the track. Get out of the house. Socialize." Desperately she clings to her routine, but becomes increasingly disoriented. She avoids her friends. She is lonely in her despair. She sits by herself for long afternoons in her sunny living room—the same room where, for 50 years, she welcomed family, friends, artists, dancers, and poets with hearty applause, unconditional love, and unabashed enthusiasm; the room where anyone with a new project was given a sumptuous meal as well as an audience on whom to present and practice. Now, Mom sits in her sunny living room thinking about her bowel movements. She records them daily while calculating how much milk of magnesia is necessary to stay regular. This is her main topic for discussion. I entertain these discussions, give her my opinion and change my mind based on her response. After all she is still my mother and I accommodate any small changes to keep from acknowledging a PROBLEM. I am content to ignore the warning signs, disallowing the accumulation of her changes the dignity of an assessment. I prefer denial.

When she says, "I'll take six milk of magnesia tablets tonight, since five didn't work last night."

I say, "Good and we'll see how that works in the morning."

Then she says, "But what if it's too much? I won't make it to the toilet in time. I'll explode!" Her anxiety grows.

"Then take five and a half," I suggest.

"But what if it's not enough? Then I'll really be constipated! Oh, what am I gonna do? What am I gonna do?"

"Okay!" I say, "Take six!" We go on to another topic until five minutes later...

"Six, Trace? You really think so?" She asks this like the world rests on my opinion. Her world apparently does. I never knew I could be so interesting. This can go on for hours if I let it.

Night terrors keep her awake. She scrawls on the backs of the file folders she uses for storing her recent calculations, "I don't want to go on. I'm a goner. It's too late. Listen to me, while I'm still sharp. Please don't let me linger. I want to die."

But I can't listen. I'm desperate to save her. Desperate to have my effervescent mother back where she belongs—in her healthy body, in her charming house surrounded by everything and everyone she loves. Now her torpid body slumps in front of me. Where is her playful spirit? Why can't we just chalk this whole thing up to a senior moment and go out for Chinese food, see a movie, split a pack of gum, apply lipstick, and paint the town?

"Mom," I say. "Listen to me. Don't give up!"

She begins seeing a psychiatrist, who informs me that in 50% of elderly people, depression is a sign of Alzheimer's. I decide that Mom's is not that kind of depression. Mom's is just depression—the curable kind. I will find the cure, because surely Mom wants it. This is a person who has always loved life. If she needs to be prodded to be the person she once was, I can do that. I know that if this depression turns out to be Alzheimer's disease or any other form of dementia, it has only one possible ending, and zero happy solutions. But for now, no one will talk about it. Certainly, not me.

The psychiatrist prescribes a round of anti-depressants. "So far, no good!" Mom uses another stock phrase to report her lack of results while shaking her head, rounding her shoulders, and bending forward in a helpless pose, like a sick toddler waiting to be lifted.

I take over the bill paying and balance her checkbook, although I insist she can still be involved. It angers me to watch her take this posture and concede defeat. How could she give in to this feeling? It is uncharacteristic. I am unaccustomed to hearing her whine.

"I'll write the checks, you address the envelopes. Don't forget the return address," I urge as we begin to conquer a pile of bills. I look back when she finishes the first envelope. The return address, in clear and columned letters, reads:

Sylvia Kravitz
619 S. Fourth St.
Philadelphia 47, Penna.

—her name and address, as she would have written it 60 years ago! This had been her South Philadelphia address when she was twenty-one and single. She lived with her aging parents and worked full time as a bookkeeper to support them.

I start trembling. Where did she get this? Is this an old envelope suddenly appearing? Why is she doing this to me?! It is a *Twilight Zone* moment. I don't show her this visiting envelope from another time. It will only confirm her fears. I feel angry as if she did it on purpose to prove her point. I can't bear to hear her say, "See I told you I'm no good!" or worse to watch her burst into tears. I do what I learned from her to do when things are too hard to face. I cover it over, attempting to convince both of us that nothing is wrong. I write the checks, balance the book, and hide the monstrous address under a label. But I can't hide my trembling—a lost beat, then recovery, arising from my chest and charging my body with a vibrating current of dread. I drop things. I can't sit still. I stutter. My body is trying to warn my mind, to shake some sense into it. "Wake up! Her mental status has changed!" Change will be the constant from now on and my jitters will continue for two and a half years of suffering, mostly. It isn't all bad, which is why I can't concede defeat in the fight against Mom's strong desire to die. It is mostly suffering because in between her bouts of hysterically screaming, "I want to die! I want to die!" and the pep chants Amity and I repeat to her as we march around the living room, "Life is worth living for, don't give it up!" and the onslaught of bowel issues, lost eye-glasses, and clean-denture obsessions— in between all of this, Mom appears:

"Trace, I miss you. What can I do for you, Sweetheart? Shall we go out for dinner? My treat!" she chirps as if a switch has been thrown, her blood begins flowing and she picks up her past life where she left off. I run along with her, when these moments come. I think magically. We giggle and fawn over the simplest things until she vanishes, forgetting it ever happened. My spirit plunges.

My brother, Myles, who lives about two hours away in Harrisburg, is concerned and frustrated as he follows Mom's changes from a distance. He suggests we take a day trip to his house. Perhaps the ride and a change of scenery will do her some good. In the past, she has enjoyed her visits, especially with her toddler grandson Austin, Myles and his wife Terry's son. Mom, as usual, is up for the trip. I arrange with Tony for Amity's care and travel with Mom to Harrisburg. Mom is in a great place mentally, and her buoyant mood continues throughout the day, as she holds Austin, sings to him, smacks her enthusiastic lips at dinner, and enjoys every moment in between. "Let's stay over," I suggest to her. There's plenty of room. She's on a roll. I want to keep this going. Perhaps the baby makes the difference, I'm thinking. I call home to share this idea with Tony and he is agreeable. Then I settle us into the guest room. Mom finds the TV remote, switches to PBS, and settles into the Ken Burns documentary on Mark Twain.

"This is fantastic! This program has so much to offer. Quick Trace, get me a pad and pencil. I want to take notes. I read *Huckleberry Finn* in junior high. You read it too. Remember?" Mom continues, "Gee, I'm really enjoying this. What great programming they have on WHYY! Trace, remind me to send them a check!"

The program ends but her enthusiasm coasts way into the night. We eventually get into bed, but she can't settle down. She is giddy as a sixth grader at her first pajama party. She suggests we raid the fridge and make sundaes. Tripping and giggling, we negotiate the darkened house. She steadies herself, her hands on the walls, fingers spread apart, she bumps into the dining room table, backs up and changes direction like one of Austin's remote controlled cars. Her laughter erupts at every wrong turn until I forge ahead to the refrigerator and light her way from the open door. She collapses on a kitchen chair and we surround ourselves with cartons of Breyer's ice cream, bowls of pretzels, M&M's and anything else I can come up with, as I ravage the refrigerator attempting to keep up with my mother's increased appetite for living.

"See if they have chocolate syrup," she insists. "Oh Trace, I don't ever want to go to sleep," she pleads with me. We stay up till four in the morning, then drop exhausted into the double bed.

Awakening at 10:00 a.m., I look over at Mom hoping to greet the person whose sparkling eyes finally shut at 4:00 a.m. "Morning, Mom! What a great night we had, huh?" Her body is stiff, dead-weight in a blanket, and she moves like a zombie, communicating with a series of grunts and an under-her-breath "Go to hell!" as I struggle to unwrap her, guide her to the bathroom and help her to dress. Stooped over her walker, she is angry and resentful as I prod her toward the kitchen for breakfast with the family. Her eyes hold nothing and there is no eye contact. She has nothing to give. The previous evening, and the spark of life that prompted it is gone. Austin avoids his grandmother when he realizes he is being ignored, and Terry guides him to his next activity. I meet Myles's misty eyes—pale blue, just like Dad's, as he helps me pack up and load Mom into the car.

"I'll call you later," I say. He nods.

Each time Mom's sparkle reappears, it is more precious, and each subsequent disappearance more devastating. Each time I am fooled and grateful to have her with me. But for the tease of these returns, I tremble. Meanwhile, back at her own home, alone at night and anxiety obsessed, she leaves envelopes around the house with cryptic messages on them. "I drove myself crazy thinking, thinking...." Perhaps she suspects we'll find them someday and understand.

At her psychiatrist's recommendation, she begins attending a mental health day-program on the campus of Friends' Hospital. A van picks her up in the morning and brings her home around dinnertime. I schedule a home health aide for the evenings. On the Friday afternoon of the first week in the day program, she calls to say, "Trace, how about if I stay overnight here at the hospital? Maybe they can help me." She sounds upbeat, like her old self.

I ask to speak with her program instructor. "What do you think? Is this a good idea?"

"Perhaps it will be good for her." She is supportive, so I cancel the aide at home and discard my plan to sleep at Mom's house on Sunday. I breathe a sigh of relief. Perhaps she'll find something hopeful, and I'll have some time off. But an hour later, Mom calls, sounding desperate.

"Trace, I don't want to stay here. Get me out of here!"

"Oh come on Mom," I say. "I thought you wanted to give it a chance. Maybe they can help you. You thought so an hour ago." I am thinking about how I cancelled the aide and re-planned my weekend. I'm about to go out to dinner with Tony and Amity. "Just give it a chance, Ma."

"If I stay here Tracy, it's the beginning of the end," Mom says.

"Aw Mom...." I just can't listen to her. Here she goes again, I think, prophesying doom. "Oh come on, Mom. I'll see you tomorrow. Have a good night. I love you. Bye."

I quickly hang up. It's a Friday night and I want to go out with my family. We choose Little Saigon Restaurant. It's a family business and the owner and his family treat us like a part of theirs, especially Amity. In fact, they call her by the name Van, since we shared that it was her Vietnamese birth name. She responds to the sound of her original name, but only when spoken by our Vietnamese family. With her slender, dexterous fingers, Amity shoves a large amount of rice noodles into her mouth, and I don't try to stop her or instruct her with a fork. In fact, her cuteness provides just another photo op for our camera-ready family. I'm feeling more normal now and glad to be out and away from Mom's problems. But the distance from her doesn't keep my anxiety, like slippery noodles, from overflowing into the evening. Did I make the right decision? Should I take her home? I am conflicted and keep considering and then pushing my thoughts aside, like the food on my plate. I eat little and take lots of pictures.

The next day, I visit Mom at the hospital and bring toiletries. I look around at the stark room. A bare bulb provides bleak light from above. She sits hunched over on a single institutional cot. The empty cinder-block walls, the stale air— — nothing there, no vestiges of her past, no souvenirs from good times, no boyfriend to mask her deficiencies. She looks up at me, eyes wide-open and desperate. She points to the underpants wrapped around her ankles. "I can't make BM!" she says.

I stare into the tormented face of her illness, recognizing it for the first time. It is, as she named it, the beginning of the end.

Cockeyed Optimism

Winter, 2002

Mom's illness has yet to be diagnosed. Her current psychiatrist, Dr. Small, a tall woman in her thirties, calls it depression. Dr. Small sits on the floor with her knees tucked under her to take Mom's blood pressure and make level eye contact when Mom is seated. "Sylvia, draw me the face of a clock and show me three p.m." Mom complies no problem. "Add this series of numbers." This is a cinch for my mother, the bookkeeper. She receives a perfect score. "Now count down from 25 to 1."

"I'm done with this idiocy!" Mom yells then snaps her mouth shut. Her exasperation signals the end of another session with Dr. Small, who increases Mom's Celexa and dismisses her. Dr. Small concludes that this is depression and nothing more. I am hopeful that whatever has happened to Mom can be cured, as the doctors tell me, through the correct protocol of medication. My personal strategy, however, is to resuscitate the cockeyed optimism that once pervaded my family's life. "Cockeyed Optimist" is the title of a song from the Rodgers and Hammerstein musical, *South Pacific*. Throughout my childhood, the sound track blasted from our Hi-Fi record player. I remember the album cover smattered with white specks, rough and peeling from a botched paint job in the living room. The LP hadn't suffered. The song describes an unrelenting naiveté, so green that it never ripens.

I remember Mom expressing her own brand of cockeyed optimism. She checked in with us every day: "Everything's great, great, great! Right?" Mom belted this like a song in a musical— bright, cheery, and with a grand smile. How could life not be great?

As it happened, Mom was great, great, great throughout her life and through ten great years of retirement—until now. Now, she is falling apart at the age of 82. Over the next couple of years, I will find out that a series of small strokes have chipped away at her brain, creating a dark and insidious depression. Multi-infarct dementia will set in. This illness will carry with it all the anger and pain that she has so successfully avoided for most of her life. But for now, I do not realize this. I do not know that this is why Mom moans with her head in her hands, "Nothing's right, nothing's right."

Mom seems to know more than the doctors or me and projects her own gloomy diagnostic commentary as the illness progresses. When I mention that "our Robyn," her niece Lily's daughter, who is a nurse, is considering flying in from abroad to see her, Mom says, "Oh, she doesn't have to come now. I'm not going anywhere. I'll suffer for a few years and then I'll die." And she'll be right about that.

As her incontinence problems increase Mom says, "Just wait. Soon I'll start smelling bad." She's right about that too. I cling to the comfort-food sentiments of my childhood, where a Tastykake chocolate cupcake and a glass of cold milk, or a Pepsi soothed all wounds.

"Don't worry, Mom. Everything will get better. I'll make it all better, just wait and see."

"Trace," she says, "you're so naïve. Don't you see what's coming?" She looks at me with eyes suddenly clear and wide-open in surprise and concern—a rare moment of clarity for her. It's as if I can read Mom's thoughts. Which are: "I know what's going to happen to me, but what will happen to Tracy? She can't face this." Again, she is right. I cannot believe that there isn't a cure for this—that I can't save her. I can't believe that she is so changed. I am angry with her for being depressed, for not coping the way she always has, for losing her optimism. I can't accept it. I am angry with myself for trying so hard to please her that I am over-extended and still unsuccessful. I am angry that she wants to die, that she would leave us with no explanation for what happened. I am angry that she isn't the grandmother she used to be—the grandmother she was to my niece and nephew. Now it's my daughter's turn, and where the hell is

Mom?? I miss my mother and want this miserable old woman to disappear. And I'm disappointed in the resources we all assumed would be here for us, if we ever needed them. I'm disappointed in the doctors, even while I take copious notes at Mom's appointments and follow every medication protocol to the T. I am disappointed with the therapy and day programs, with my brothers and my cousins and my large, extended family suddenly scarce. Nothing and no one is working as expected. But I confront Mom's gloom and doom with my own brand of cockeyed optimism, applying Band-Aids to every new trauma.

"Don't worry, Mom. We'll figure this out." This just releases her anger and robs her of discretion.

"You're so full of shit, Tracy!" My once literate, cultured, happy-go-lucky mother reproaches me.

Mom is losing her mind and she knows it, even though the rest of us are hanging on to her moments of clarity as the rule rather than the exception. I have a vision of myself and my brothers as children hanging on to Mom's ample, competent arms as she juggles work and family. But the reality is, we are grown, scattered, and clinging to a memory. I consider the options and suggest assisted-living. At least, she won't be home alone.

Mom moves willingly to The Protestant Home. It's nearby, and has a pool for the lap swimming that she and I both enjoy. Even though she is Jewish, we don't think the name or the mostly Christian population will be a problem for her. She has lived and worked with people from diverse backgrounds. Mom always fits in. Also, this assisted living facility is just blocks away from the government compound where she was employed for 25 years. Perhaps she'll run into some of the old gang from work. My brother, Myles, moves her into the freshly painted efficiency apartment. He brings the queen bed, headboard, and TV from her bedroom at home, as well as the reclining chair from the living room. He even brings the small refrigerator that she kept in the basement from when Myles lived there as a teenager. We're trying to keep things as familiar and comfortable as possible. Although we insist, "this is just a trial, we'll see how she likes it, we don't have to sell the house right away," this is the beginning of the end of her home, and I'm glad I'm not there to see it. I'm at my house with 30 five-year-olds making a birthday party for Amity; knowing how much Mom (my mother of previous years) would have wanted to be there.

Meanwhile, Mom seems to be making a good adjustment in her new home. She swims, takes walks on the grounds, and has met the neighbors. Within a month or two, she says, "Sell my house. I don't want to worry about it anymore." Her home of 52 years was her pride and joy. She and Dad savored every stage of its construction back in 1950. Full of the remains of everything that ever meant anything to her, her house now seems to be just another burden to leave behind—a remnant from a fading life. I do as I'm told and contract with the realtor she suggests.

However, The Protestant Home turns out to be the wrong choice. She hates the food, stops eating, has nothing to do, and no one she wants to see. She complains, "I feel like I'm in jail." I encourage her to attend activities. When I really look into it, I find that they are sparse, but we check out a crafts class together to get her started. We enter the multi-purpose room and survey the long table where stooped-over, ancient women in bridge chairs on either side, passively await instruction. Elmer's glue, safety scissors, construction paper and balls of yarn cover the table. It smells like kindergarten—laced with mothballs.

Mom turns to me and whispers, "Trace, can you believe I ended up in a place like this?" As usual, her thoughts mirror mine.

"Let's get out of here, Mom. How 'bout Chinese food?" I whisper back. We turn and escape. Mom beats me to the door.

Initially, she swam every day taking advantage of her "new home with a pool." Recently, "something happened," she tells me. "I was changing my clothes in the basement locker room after swimming, I forgot where I was! I thought I was back at the 'Y' but I didn't know anyone. I was naked, shivering, and crying on the bench, when a couple of the more together women found my clothes, helped me dress, and took me back to my room. I'm not going there by myself anymore." She isolates herself most of the time now, embarrassed by the state of her mind and not wanting to be "assisted" by her peers. To help her feel less closed in, I suggest a trip to the art museum.

"We'll spend the day together, just like we used to." She agrees, but I put it off for a few days, favoring her doctoring schedule and my other responsibilities.

She comments, "You promise me all these great things, and then you don't follow through."

"I'm trying as hard as I can," I say. Her criticism tortures me because I spend most of my time trying to make things great for her. Before her illness, disappointment in me was not something she would ever express, even if I deserved it. It wasn't in her make up to reproach me. She preferred not to hurt my feelings. As for her own feelings, she used her inner resources to get over disappointments and move on. She could make herself happy by chewing gum and turning on the radio.

Now it seems her emotional resources have totally dried up. She wants to die, and yet her whole life was shaped by a never-say-die attitude. She is a child of immigrants who picked themselves up, dusted themselves off, and were productive and upbeat for every long, hard day that God gave them. So, what is this thing that first gnawed at her and has now whacked her over the head "turning my brains to molasses," as she repeats to doctors and friends—another one of her stock phrases. Worry lines her face. Anxiety strips her of pleasure. Desperate to save herself, she stays up all night attempting word puzzles, Jumbles, from the newspaper, to exercise her mind, and avoid the nightmares she can't separate from when awakening.

She makes lists on the backs of envelopes: "Cancel credit card, cell phone. Get Tracy's name on bank accounts." She wants to cancel everything, get rid of things, so she won't worry about them. She thinks the less she has, the less she'll lose. She begins hiding from friends and family, not answering her phone. When she can pull herself together to go out, she asks her peers, "Do you ever get depressed? Do you ever cry first thing in the morning and have a hard time leaving your bedroom?" She'd never had. Never, ever one day of her life when she didn't just "hop to it!" So, what the hell is happening now?

Now her body is bent over. Her head oscillates back and forth. When she stands, her quivering fists are balled in anger and her face wears a permanent scowl. Her walk is as crooked as her expression, as she wanders the halls of her new home in search of a sandwich or something to do. I take her out to the art museum and she complains the whole drive there. "How will I get around? It's too much trouble. You take on too much. I can't understand anything anymore, anyway. Your driving makes me crazy. There's nowhere to park. How will I walk the steps?" She'd never been a complainer. Now every activity provokes deep anxiety. Yet, despite her discomfort, I know she still wants to try. She climbs the steps and we borrow a wheelchair from the museum. We take in the Degas exhibit. She listens to the audio-taped lecture, although she says she can hardly hear it through the earphones. I wheel her past canvas after canvas of Degas' ballet dancers.

"You used to have postcards of so many of these paintings taped to the dining room wall, Mom. Remember? That's how I know them!" After this exhibit, we go to the museum cafeteria for coffee and chocolate chip cookies. When she's finished, she stands erect, busses our table, wipes it clean with her napkin, and instead of sitting in it, she pushes the wheelchair.

"I don't think I really need this." She waves at the air in front of her, as if to push away the curtain of the last six months. We return to the gallery rooms and peruse the rest of the Impressionists paintings. Mom begins to reminisce. "Such beauty and grace. I miss the ballet and the orchestra. Remember the exceptional films we saw here, and those great dinners afterwards? Y'know, this is where Daddy and I shared our first kiss—right here on the steps of the art museum back in 1946...."

"I remember the story, Mom. And the Exceptional Film Society, and those great meals we had after the movies. Y'know, we can still go to the orchestra. I'll get tickets. And let's have dinner out tonight, my treat." It's not just generosity on my part. I need this reprieve. For dinner, we stop at a Chinese restaurant. As she dunks fried noodles in duck sauce, she chats about what a great time we've had, and how lucky we are as Philadelphians to have such a great treasure as the Philadelphia Museum of Art "in our own backyard." She eats her shrimp in lobster sauce as if she hasn't eaten in weeks because she hasn't. Finally, I take her back to her room at The Protestant Home. Not to my house, because I have somewhere to go that night and the bed is too high and she might roll off and I don't have a sitter and so many other reasons. So, she returns to her new home where she slumps in her chair and forgets about every great thing that happened that day.

The following afternoon, I stop by her room and find her still in bed. "Get the hell out of here! Let me die!!" she greets me. I find her hand under the covers and hold it. Then, quickly, I pull mine back.

"Ouch! Goddamn it, Mom!! You bit me!" I begin to cry.

"Just put me somewhere," she says.

"Yeah, Mom. If only I knew where."

Now my head is in my own trembling hands. I live in a world of "if onlys." Night and day, my mind never stops thinking up grand solutions to a problem that just doesn't have one. If only, I'd taken her home with me that evening after the museum. If only, I could take her home to her house, where now the azaleas are in bloom and the roses are budding. "Perfect to attract a buyer," says the realtor.

If only, I could leave her at the art museum in some kind of designated assisted living wing—admiring ballerinas and lingering by Monet's garden pond. She would be constantly inspired and happy, and we could go back to life as usual. If only, I could look ahead with cockeyed optimism, but I am growing less green.

Assisted Living

Spring, 2002

Assisted living is assisted dying. My mother— lover of art, culture, good food, and flowing conversation— is drying up before my eyes, in a space designed to make life easier through assistance with daily living skills. Regardless of all the pictures we hang on the closet and bathroom doors, the favorite books and mementos on the shelves, the wide selection of films and home movies on video, the small refrigerator stocked with Pepsi, the microwave with popcorn in the corner, and all the other ways my brothers and I turn her new room into our collective dream of a simplified, yet happy retirement existence, to Mom, it's just a place to die.

She is clinically depressed, has anxiety attacks, and psychotic episodes. She can't be in her own home alone. But this room, just a shout from the nurses' station, holds nothing for her and she no longer has the resources to make something out of nothing. Her window faces west and her room is high enough above the city to enjoy the amber/orange sky at sunset. I like visiting her this time of day for the view.

"Mom, remember when the boys and I were kids? You'd drive us the 60 miles to the Atlantic City beach early on summer mornings. We wanted to go bike riding on the boardwalk before breakfast. We'd watch the sunrise on the way to the shore. I remember that pink sky and how you'd make us feel so lucky to catch the moment when the sun appeared— like it was ours alone, in the car with us— like it was worth it to get up that early, and it was just the beginning of the greatest day in the world, because we were there when it started. And they were great days— running in and out of the ocean, eating and sleeping on the warm sand. Remember how we'd bury you and then you'd have to go in that cold ocean to get rinsed off? The only reason I was willing to pack up and leave at the end of the day was because of the fuss you'd make over the sun setting in front of us on the drive home."

"Look at that gorgeous, orange sky!' you'd say. 'We are so lucky! It's always there waiting to welcome us home.' And then we'd stop for ice cream, and watch the sun go down."

"I don't remember," Mom says. Her lack of emotion stuns me, as much as the effusion of her earlier years was fuel. Now, Mom sees only darkness on the horizon. She, who taught me to stop and appreciate the light, seems blind to it.

I had begun the process of selling her house and relinquishing her responsibilities to clear her mind of worry. But the things she worried about were also the things that had brought her the most joy. In this new environment, both worry and joy are diminished. I am still determined to find in her some remnant of the person she was, and to keep that alive. Regardless of how lost she may feel, I am not ready to let her disappear. I simply cannot let go of the spark that was Mom.

I have my own regime for assisting her living. After dropping off five-year-old Amity at kindergarten each day, I drive for forty minutes arriving at my mother's room bearing shopping bags of chicken soup, soft pretzels, and Tastykakes. I stash my packages in the small fridge and clap my hands indicating the beginning of our exercise regime. "Okay Mom, bend and stretch, reach for the stars! There goes Jupiter, here comes Mars!" I stretch and rotate my body, palms facing the ceiling. She lifts her arms, opens her hands in front of her chest, and rotates from the waist. Mom silently follows everything I do. Her old self was a firm believer in exercise. Today she is trying hard to remain that person, without any of the passion or energy that defined her.

"Touch your toes, Mom, and repeat after me, one, two, three." I bend at the waist, dipping toward my toes.

"One, two, three," she repeats lurching forward, looking and sounding like a robot. Regardless, her response encourages me as I add more tasks to our routine.

"Hands on your hips, Mom, bounce forward, two, three; side, two, three; back, two, three…" This regime is good for my stressed-out body. Mom's face remains impassive. For her, it's an exercise in patience. "Okay, time for the fitness center!" Mom follows me out of her room, toward the elevator. She makes no eye contact with her neighbors.

The fitness center is clean, brightly lit and hardly used. Mom is willing as I assist her climb onto a stationary bike. She sits erect on the stationary bike, peddling endlessly in a remembered pattern. She just won't initiate or end the ride, so I leave her to peddle for twenty minutes while I take advantage of the otherwise unused equipment.

We go out to lunch, and then I settle her in for a nap, before leaving to collect Amity from aftercare. While driving to and from, I am on my cell phone managing Mom's healthcare and my photography business, and calling my brothers to argue about what else we should do. I always call Myles at this time to give him a progress report. The forty-minute drive goes quickly. "So what did the doctor say?" Myles asks.

"Well, she's trying Celexa during the day and Seroquel at night. Just waiting for it to kick in."

"Turning Mom into a drug addict isn't the answer! They should take her off of everything. When I talk to her in the morning she's fine. It's after the drugs kick in that she has a problem."

"That's a theory Myles, but if she were fine every morning, she could be home alone. We wouldn't be having this conversation." Our repetitive back and forth settles on nothing and degenerates into anger and grief. When I drive through a dead zone after thirty minutes, I am grateful to lose our connection. Neither one of us bothers to call back, we've had enough for one day.

All this caretaking activity is causing me to lose weight and develop muscles. That's the good part. The harder part is that my mind is divided: when I'm with my mother, I feel guilty for missing valuable moments of my daughter's childhood; when I'm with my daughter, I feel guilty for leaving Mom alone.

I begin bringing Amity to swim with "Bubbe" at her pool. This is a great way to take a small child to a retirement home, making it fun. The vending machines are a fascinating new experience for Amity, coating our visits with sugar and salt. The comfort and joy to be found in potato chips, chocolate cupcakes, and Pepsi is passed on to the next generation.

The pool water is a little too warm for me at eighty-eight degrees, especially when I glance around at the residents and consider the possible incontinence. But it's perfect for Amity's small body, accustoming to water. It gives her the confidence, without the shivers, to take her first swim strokes. The familiar scenario of the swimming pool— the clear, blue water, the light streaming in through the windows, our laughter bouncing off the walls and spirits buoyant as we splash, even the thick smell of chlorine seems to lighten Mom up. It clears her head. But when I see Mom, across from Amity and me in the shallow end, submerge and not resurface, I lunge toward the other side of the four-foot line to rescue her. I leave my daughter alone and clinging to the metal steps— halfway into the pool. "Hold onto the steps Am," I yell, as I reach Mom, grab the back of her head, and raise it above water. How could she forget to lift her head?

"You've saved my life, Tracela!" she gasps, but her eyes sparkle. "Let's get dressed and go out for pizza." I gather Amity who does not want to leave. Her arms are folded across her chest, her shoulders droop, her tiny lips have turned blue and are pursed in a frown. She is still on the steps, submerged to her waist

"Why did you leave me?"

"Bubbe needed my help, Am. She forgot to lift her head!"

"Bubbe knows how to swim, Mom!"

"Soon you'll be a better swimmer than Bubbe," I hug her shivering body. "Now let's go have some pizza. You must be starving." In the locker room, Amity is sullen and distracted. She keeps stealing glances at her new, "needy" Bubbe. Sharing a time slot with these two is not going to be easy.

"Bubbe could've drowned, Am." Amity does not buy it. Once in the car, Mom asks for her favorite radio station, pulls out a pack of gum, shares it with Amity, and applies her lipstick. Amity's mood adjusts as well.

"Nothing like a good-old-fashioned New England Pizza to revive you," Mom chirps. She loves the New England Pizza parlor that was walking distance from her home. She was one of their first customers when they opened in 1965. Going there tonight to celebrate life is a return to familiarity and fun. She orders milkshakes and pizza all around, insisting it's her treat. For that evening, she seems unbound by her fate. But the next day her depression returns, her shoulders fall forward, her head sinks to her lap. She wants nothing to do with anyone. The isolation of her room again becomes her crypt.

On weekends, I photograph weddings for a living. As I document the most beautiful days of life, the poetic toasts, and the outpouring of appreciation between parents and children, I remember what a joyful family mine had once been. As I make portraits of dreamy-eyed couples, I wonder, "Do they understand the fragility of happiness?" I travel in my mind back to the ebullient speeches my mother, the toastmistress, used to make at such occasions. "I'm so thrilled to be here celebrating our beautiful family...." I can't go off in thought for very long before my cell phone rings. Mom is still able to manage the phone, although she no longer says, "Sweetheart! How are you?" A hopeless, helpless, soulless voice calls out to me from a dark canyon.

"What am I gonna do? What am I gonna do?"

"Gotta go. Call you back," I whisper. On a Saturday morning wedding photography gig, as I position myself in the center aisle of the church, ready and waiting to capture the entrances of the major players, Mom's first ring on my cell phone usually arrives just when the bridesmaids do— a false cue before the first chord of the organ. I learn to shut the damn thing off, although I feel guilty and worried throughout the vows. If it's a Catholic Mass, I can exit the church, take a picture of the program in natural light, and call Mom back, knowing I have an hour before my next shot. "So what's happening, Mom?"

"I want to die."

"I'd like you to live, comfortably."

"What am I going to do? What am I going to do?"

"Get involved. Exercise."

"I feel like I'm in jail."

"Go outside. You like that."

"With you, I'll go. I'm not capable by myself."

"Can't anyone take you?"

"I'm all alone here. What am I going to do?"

"I'll find someone to take you. Gotta go. Call you back later."

I return to the mass and find comfort sitting in the last pew. I quietly sing along: "Christ has died, Christ is risen, Christ will come again." I close my eyes, fold my hands in my lap and escape into the rise and fall of the notes, "a A MEN, A a men, aA A a men." The familiar symmetry of the hymn lulls me, simplifying and settling my thoughts, even while the cell phone vibrates furiously against my right thigh. But when the music stops, my frazzled brain returns to its constant reiteration of all the possible ways I might rescue my mother from oblivion. Taking her home to her house is out of the question. It brings us back to the original problem of round-the-clock care. Even if it works for a while, there will come a day sooner rather than later when there will be another move. Besides, the house is already under contract. This is the logical part of my mind speaking. But then the optimist speaks: Why not call off the sale and move her back home? The house isn't packed up yet. After all, it's where she is most comfortable. It's a relentless inner dialogue— a broken record of rumination.

Over lunch the following week, Mom says, "I want you to go to my house and get your china out of the basement. It's in a box labeled "Tracy". I don't want it to get lost. I've been saving it for you all these years. I want you to have it."

"Don't worry. I'll get it when I pack up the house. We still have some time."

"I want you to get it now. I'm worried about it," she insists. I drive us to her house.

"Stay in the car. I'll go inside and get the china. I'll be out in a second," I insist.

I don't think she wants to go in. There are steps to climb. I come up from the basement through the kitchen into the dining room with cartons piled high in front of my face. Out of the corner of my eye, I notice Mom seated, hands folded in front of her at the dining room table. It's like an apparition— a visitation from a recently departed soul. She had climbed the stairs. In her large hazel eyes, I see the light of this house, the chandelier's reflection of this dining room— her art books, her children, her sisters, her pictures on the wall, a table set for brunch. Wide-eyed, she acknowledges a lifetime and its loss. She looks to me like a condemned prisoner aware of her sins and yet unjustly sentenced.

"Look what I have to give up!" Mom extends her plump, wide hand across the landscape that had been her life and the table where she had hosted so many celebrations. And there I am, carrying out the china. I stop and put the boxes down. We embrace and weep for our loss. In this moment, she is in her body, in her mind, and in her house for the last time.

My brothers and I begin packing up Mom's home. We do it separately, never seeing each other at the house where we lived together with our parents until adulthood. Familiar handwriting comforts me when I see Myles and Terry's labels— "middle room closet, bedroom dresser drawers, etc." in marker on the cardboard boxes they've packed, taped and piled in the corners of each room. Lanse, Bonnie, and their son Joe load what's left of the furniture into a truck, hauling it off to a storage container— an emotionally soothing pit stop before the dumpster. We never talk to each other directly about a strategy. We communicate through the familiar handwriting on boxes in otherwise empty rooms, each picking up where the other has left off.

I arrive for my last day of packing and park on the side of the house next to the patio and the front door. I stare at the entrance from my car. When their house was under construction in 1950, Mom and Dad had insisted on having the main entrance of their corner "row home" townhouse on the side, unlike the rest of the houses on the block. It secluded the patio and front door on one side and allowed them their own little corner with a garden. They planted some trees, azalea bushes and even a grape vine. They surrounded it all with a black metal railing. This was their masterpiece and the first and only house either of them would ever own. I stare up at their house, pick up my phone, and call my brother Myles.

"Does she really have to give up her house? Can't we just bring her home? Won't she be better off? Can we afford the help? Can we just stop the sale, regardless of what it costs or what problems it causes? How long will that give us until she needs more care? Ever? Maybe never! The azaleas are blooming, now!" I'm feeling desperate and I know that this is my last futile attempt at stopping a runaway train. Myles sympathizes, starts calculating our losses, and then stops.

"We'll move her to Paul's Run where her friends are, we'll get her a nice apartment, and furnish it with stuff we have from the house. She'll like it better there." He talks me down and we close with a new plan.

I enter the house to vacuum and sweep every room from top to bottom: the three second-floor bedrooms including the small one that was mine, it's purple/pink shag rug still intact; and the hall bath where the six of us half-dressed, my mother and father, me and my brothers, Sheldon, Lanse, and Myles had crowded around two sinks at the last second before school and work for so many years. I sweep down the hallway and vacuum the carpeted steps to the living room. I remember tumbling down them as a toddler and hitting my head on the built-in mirrored cabinet that Dad crafted at the bottom. I remember practically carrying my cancer-ridden father down these stairs on his final descent, ten years ago. I quickly vacuum the living room, dining room, sweep the kitchen and basement steps. I stop and stand above the room where we as children, teenagers and young adults carried on all the hidden and unsupervised activities that every basement remembers. I sweep and muse through the laundry room to the garage where indelible oil stains remember racing car engines built and re-built by my brother, Lanse. These stains refuse to be swept away. I realize that this house will remember us no matter who sleeps in the master bedroom or what food is served for brunch in the dining room. We've left our mark. I sweep the last vestiges of our family out the garage door and leave this house sparkling clean, quiet, and empty— exactly as it hasn't been for 52 years. The house is sold. I attend the closing, burst into tears as I shake the new owner's hand and leave with the realtor who tells me not to be embarrassed by my sobbing. He sees it all the time. It's very common. I'm not embarrassed. It's hardly a fitting eulogy.

Mom is unhappy and we decide to make a change. When I suggest that she come and live with me, Mom replies, "I don't want to be a burden, just put me somewhere." But I can't just put her somewhere, when I see the result.

"So, you don't like where you are? Don't worry," I say. "I'll find you a better place. I'll find a resort for you—assisted living in the Borscht Belt!"

"Sounds delicious!" She cracks a smile for an instant. She almost laughs. I notice that she is still capable of good humor under the right circumstances. I just have to find them. I begin gathering information and making the phone calls. I set up an interview with Paul's Run Retirement Community for the following month.

Within a week, Mom slips while rushing to the bathroom. Her hip is broken. She is taken to the hospital. It's a Saturday and I am photographing a wedding in Princeton, New Jersey. I call my brother, Lanse, and he is there for her, post-operative. It goes well. Her body is still relatively healthy. I visit on Sunday.

"Trace, take a look at these pictures from Bryce Canyon National Park. I feel like I'm in Utah, just looking at them! It's just great!"

Mom sits up in bed, bright-eyed and relaxed as she peruses through an album of old photos. "There's nothing like travel to broaden the mind," she chirps, never mentioning her fall, the surgery or the pin that now rejoins her hip. But within a few days, she is transferred to a room at the rehabilitation center on the same campus as her assisted-living apartment.

"I thought you were getting me out of here, Tracy!" She is back in jail and I am her keeper. But the prescribed physical therapy turns out to be even better for her mind than it is for her body. Whether she wakes up depressed or hopeful, the activity of going to the PT room, interacting with the same, interested therapists, and having a set routine of daily exercise, does wonders for her spirit, at least for that period of the day. She performs for her teachers. After three weeks, coinciding with the amount of days Medicare covers the cost of a rehab, Mom is deemed rehabilitated. On the last day of physical therapy, she rises to her newly pronounced status returning the compliment to the staff, "You gals are all so great! So helpful! I want to thank you. I wish I could bake you a tray of my world-famous k'mish bread!" And to me she says, "Gee Trace, I'll be walking in no time!"

I recognize this sudden burst of enthusiasm. I'm no longer fooled by it, although I still enjoy it with her. I begin to see a pattern. Every ten days or so, it is as if the curse lifts and Mom, my real mom, is back for a few hours charming everyone with her warmth and optimism. Then she goes back to her room in assisted living, sinks into her chair and deflates. As do I. Post rehab, I continue my quest for the perfect solution. The admissions officer at Paul's Run interviews and admits Mom. She is scheduled to move-in a month later. We drive the short distance there a few weeks prior to leave a security deposit. I park and write the check in the car with Mom beside me, so she can be a part of this decision. At the sight of the amount we are spending, Mom flips. "Take me back to my room, Tracy! I'm not moving here! Put the goddamn check away and tell them to cancel everything. I'm not moving! Don't sign that check! Don't sign it! Don't! I'm staying where I am! I insist you listen! Go in and cancel everything!"

"Mom, you have friends here." I'm trembling.

"I don't care!"

"But Mom, you're not happy where you are so we're, we're, we're making a change." I stutter.

"Yes I am! Let me be. Listen to me, Tracy. Let me be. I refuse to move!" Mom screams and her eyes bulge. I don't sign the check. I put away the checkbook, go into the admissions office, and do as I am told. We drive back to the Protestant Home in silence. Since the surgery, Mom depends on a walker. Despite all her physical therapy, she walks almost prostrate to the floor, pushing the walker ahead as if it were a wheelbarrow full of bricks, instead of just a rolling crutch. Nothing works for us the way it's supposed to. I recognize that I'm getting more and more depressed, and consider taking the anti-depressants that I've been doling out to Mom. They're not working for her; perhaps they will for me. But, then I get a better idea. Mom's older and last surviving sibling, Lena, twelve years her senior, is in an assisted living facility in Florida. She is now 95, but her mind is sharp. Recently, she chose to sell her condo and sign up at Heritage Park Retirement Village in Delray Beach, not far from where she lived for the past 25 years. At home, Lena was starting to feel lonely and fearful at night, and thought she could use the extra help. She has adapted well at Heritage Park, likes the routine, and has found women with whom she plays canasta. She is thrilled by the idea of her kid sister coming to live with her, although she has heard that Sylvia is "having problems."

"Nothing we can't handle together," Lena assures me by phone from Florida. Lena always helped Mom. When Lena was 24, single, and working, Mom was only twelve.

Lena gave her the money for her first theater ticket, kindling Mom's lifelong romance with the theater. Lena helped my parents throughout the years, as they struggled to make ends meet. She and her husband, Harry, amassed a small fortune in the cutlery business, literally keeping their noses to the grindstone for 50 years. They never had children. Mom showed Lena and her four other older sisters how to live beyond work. Unlike her older sisters, Mom learned to ride a bike, swim, and play tennis. She loved opera and travel. She exposed her sisters to life's pleasures. Although they were never as experimental, the sisters loved and indulged Mom's playful spirit. Bringing the two remaining sisters together again at life's end seems like a grand solution because Lena is running out of money. She never thought she would live to be 95, outliving her neighbors and her cash. She used to dream about leaving a little something to her many nieces and nephews. She'd make lists late into the night of how much would go to this one and that one. It gave her great satisfaction to think these plans through. But now she is paying rent and living off the dwindling proceeds from the sale of her condo and a small Social Security income. Her Social Security does not match the cost of assisted living. Mom, on the other hand, just recently became disabled. She has a pension from 30 years of government work, (five accumulated from before she was married,) her house has just sold, and her Social Security income is greater than Lena's. What's more, assisted living costs less in Florida. Money lasts longer there. This solution looks better and better. Mom, at 83, will provide for Lena. Lena, at 95, will now show Mom how to live. "Assisted living with Aunt Lena," I'm thinking. "This might just work!"

    The logistics of taking a depressed, demented, and physically handicapped 83-year-old woman from Philadelphia to Delray Beach are daunting. But sunny Florida always held a fresh-squeezed allure: orange juice and ocean breezes, every day a new start. I feel revitalized by the very thought. But Mom keeps changing her mind. On a good day, she'll announce, "I'm going to throw away this walker in Florida. I'll just use a cane." However, a more typical response is, "So, I'll die there." When she calls to say, "Listen Trace, I can't go to Florida. Lena's not used to the smell of my BM," I decide to stop listening to her.

The bowel obsession started while she was still living at home. She became afraid to leave the house lest she lose control. This was a valid concern, as she was more aware than any of us about her new physiological development. Wearing Depends controls the symptoms, but the anxiety around the problem is not so easily managed. Anticipating an afternoon at the theater is more stressful than the pleasure she might derive from actually being there. When I convince her to attend a show with me, she insists on an aisle seat and on lining the car with bed pads. She hasn't had a mishap, although that possibility is all she can talk about on the way. Once the curtain rises the anxiety around the problem disappears, usually until the next day.

Most of my family, including my patient and sympathetic husband Tony, thinks I am crazy to undertake the trip, but I'm desperate for this to work. Cousin Sandee calls to weigh in on the discussion. "Believe me Trace, you'll never get your mother on a plane! She'll freak out at the airport and then where will you be?"

"She's right, Tracy," Tony agrees. "I'm glad I'm not the only one thinking this. How in the world will you get her onto an airplane when some days she won't even lift her head? And Lena is 95! What if she dies? Then your mother will be alone in Florida!

"Lena's not going anywhere," I counter. "Have you talked to her lately? She's already pricing twin beds for the two of them!" Myles supports my decision. My brother is as emotionally desperate for a cure as I am. Besides, we're our mother's children. We're optimistic.

I convince Mom to travel to Florida with me and give the new situation a try. On the morning of departure, she passively follows my lead barely opening her eyes as I drug her, dress her, settle her into the car, and make the transfers from car to airport and wheelchair to plane. I feel the eyes of the other passengers on us as I prod and push her down the narrow aisle of the plane. I hold her up in the back by the waistband of her pants, while she drags her feet along. I drop her into her seat and fall into mine, exhausted.

As the plane lifts, so does her disposition. She pulls out a pack of gum and offers me a stick. I take it and chew along with her, even though it's Freedent, for denture wearers. She flags the flight attendant. "We'll have two Pepsis, please. Don't forget the pretzels," she teases. She throws back her head and chugs her drink like she is already on Delray Beach. I see a sparkle in her eyes that I imagine flight attendants are accustomed to seeing in the faces of passengers embarking on vacation. Mom looks hopeful. My spirit soars with hers on this great day in the sky. It helps not to think about the emotional crash that just as often follows a buoyant mood.

Florida—The Fresh Squeeze

January, 2003

We're snapping our fingers and clacking our gum to the big-band music of the 1940s, as Mom and I swing down Route 95 toward Delray Beach and Aunt Lena. Within the protective bubble of a rental car on cruise control, we feel secure and upbeat. In suspended animation, we suspend our expectations and underlying anxiety. The past six months up north seems as irrelevant and out-of-mind as our heavy coats, stashed away in the far recesses of the trunk. The relentless noonday Florida sun pours in through the windows, sears our limbs, and competes for our pleasure with frosty blasts of air conditioning. Mom relaxes beside me in her bucket seat, indulging the familiar, summery feeling. An occasional palm tree presses through the landscape of this humdrum highway, advertising the good times to come. We stop at a welcoming station for some fresh-squeezed OJ. I sip the chilly enzymes from a Dixie cup, remembering Mom in her heyday instructing us each morning before school, "Drink some orange juice. It washes down the *schmutz*!" I allow this liquid sunshine to burn the edges of my dry, cracked lips, coat my cottony tongue, and wash down six months of *schmutz*.

Our arrival at Heritage Park is sweet as pecan pie with ice cream. The bile in my stomach melts in an instant. Aunt Lena is jubilant. She greets us at the front door of the retirement community, with her friends surrounding her. Mom steps out of the car by herself. The sisters kiss and hold onto each other, squealing, and shaking their heads in disbelief. Soaked with tears of gratitude, they bask in the applause of the crowd. Aunt Lena stands erect at four-feet-ten inches. Mom has withered down to five feet. The two of them, holding each other up, are like a short, squat nucleus in the middle of a growing circle of adoring light. Reserves from decades in the sun are beamed at them from browned, leather-skinned smiles. Boney, trembling hands grab and hug me, as I move through the crowd. Weathered faces whisper, "You done good!"

I feel rescued. Finally, the nightmare is over. Leave it to Aunt Lena to extend home and heart to Mom at this time. The hugging, the familiar touch of sister to sister after such a long drought of illness, and Lena's familiar expressions and mannerisms anchor us. I'm thinking this must be what it's like to arrive in heaven after the hell of illness, with your loved ones standing around clapping, and all the pain and torment of life behind you. I don't think I've ever thought about heaven before.

"There's nothing wrong with her!" Aunt Lena announces to the crowd and me, sizing Mom up in a second. "Everyone here uses a walker. That's fine! Our Sylvie fits right in." Lena's brown eyes shine. In her perched, knowing smile, I see recognition and self-affirmation. Lena knows better than all those doctors up north and even more than Sylvie's worried kids. To me, Lena's smile says, "What on Earth is everyone so worried about? Yes, she looks older and slower, but this is Florida. So, what else is new? Now Sylvie's one of us!" Lena couldn't be happier and more relieved. Mom seems to feel a sense of home here with Lena, which she hasn't felt since she gave up her own.

I stay with them for two more days and hire an aide to help Mom bathe, dress, and medicate after my departure. Mom seems willing to fit in, but her bowels hesitate. Without a house, car or social life to worry about, constipation soars to the top of her list of concerns. "How can you leave me when I haven't made BM in three days?" Mom cries.

"You'll be fine once you settle in. The staff and Aunt Lena will help you," I counter, hoping she will hang on to these words of comfort in my absence.

Once the initial elation of our arrival dies down, her level of anxiety heightens. She is nervous about being "abandoned" by me in Florida. I arrange for a visiting nurse to arrive on the following day and reserve a seat for myself on the next flight home. Lena makes it clear that she is ready, willing, and able to take over for me. Mom will simply follow her around all day. They'll have a great time. I steal the book, *We Were the Mulvaneys*, by Joyce Carol Oates, from the shelves of the Heritage Park library and leave for the airport. On the plane, I relax and think of nothing but this once-loving, stable family now falling apart. It's comforting to see a family in worse shape than mine.

Thus, begins my therapy. I explore a whole new genre of books about great lives and families headed for disaster. Reading such stories helps me feel less ashamed of my mother's condition, and gives me a community to which I can feel superior. Each time my mother loses control of another daily living skill, whether the ability to hold a coherent conversation or the ability to hold her urine, I feel ashamed along with her. I'm looking forward to some time without her. At home, I get busy with the neglected aspects of my life–my child, my marriage, my business.

My first night alone, Mom calls me. "Trace! I'm talking to everybody, here. I saw a wonderful show. Lena didn't go, but the gang showed me how to get back to our room. Everyone is fabulous! But how will I drive? I want to go to the beach and out to dinner. Where's my car, anyway?" I want to believe that this is how she will feel every day. I don't question her enhanced affect, or remind her that she gave up driving last year, when she started to feel unstable. Instead, I explain about the shuttle service freeing people of responsibility for cars. Besides, we have cousins in the area.

"They'll be more than happy to take you to dinner," I encourage. We close affectionately.

Tony notices my mood of delight after the conversation. "Guess your mom's having a good day," he quips. Despite my prior experience and decreased proximity, my optimism still rises and falls with Mom's. Tony has just spent the last four days managing Amity and our business, alone. He admits to me that he is not built for this. He yearns for stability and a return to how things used to be. This is starting to feel like a major fork in the road for us, rather than just a detour. But, I'm not thinking about it.

Lena is already planning the move to a larger apartment with a view. She suggests I talk to "our Denny," my cousin who delivers furniture for a living, about a set of twin beds that he can get wholesale. Life seems back on keel. I promise Lena I'll call Denny in the morning.

Busy in my office all morning, I plan to make calls during lunch. Instead, I receive a call from Judy, the Heritage Park administrator. "I hope you've got a round-trip ticket Tracy, for your mother!" I tremble at Judy's tone.

"What happened?" I ask.

"We've been in Lena's room all morning. We've had every person who works here trying to get your mother out of bed. Lena is frantic! The visiting nurse is here with the enema and your mother won't let her near. Your mother tried to bite the nurse!" says Judy. "If I didn't have you to call, I'd commit her to a psychiatric hospital right now!"

My trembling is never too far away, eager for its next opportunity. With the shaking comes fear and a sense of catastrophe. Most of my decisions are made from this state of emergency. I feel scolded by Judy, and ashamed for my mother, our family and myself. And yet, I had told Judy about Mom's depression before we made the trip, and about her erratic behavior. At that time, Judy took it lightly, said everyone just needed a little extra love and care. Judy was most likely thinking about Lena's finances and that Mom was her meal ticket. But now Mom is not worth the trouble, and Judy wants her out. Judy's tone with me has changed. It seems we've betrayed her. We've brought disorder to Heritage Park. Nobody likes us anymore. We are free-falling further downward with no end in sight.

I grab *The Human Stain*, by Philip Roth, new and unstained from my bookshelf, and leave for the airport and the now-familiar flight to Florida.

Of course, by dinnertime, when I arrive at Heritage Park, Mom is out of bed, cooperative, and happy to see me.

"Hi Trace! Let's go out tonight. I'd love to take a drive—maybe see the ocean."

"Cool, you're on," I say, as if I live down the block and just happened to drop in.

The night breezes in a Southern Florida winter carry the scent of the clean, salted air for miles. I take Mom out for a short ride around town, five miles west of the ocean. This cruise feels as soothing to me as a day at the beach. "I could get used to this," I say. Mom agrees, as if we're on vacation. My mind actually entertains the outrageous notion of uprooting my life to move down here with her, if it will help.

"Let's get some ice cream," I suggest, relinquishing my thoughts and conversation to but one focus—crunchy chocolate sprinkles blanketing cool vanilla cream, spreading and dissolving across the vast seascape of my tongue. I pull up to the window of the local dairy bar where such simple desires are easily satisfied. With nothing else to engage us but this, we're both content. We're discovering that even while the mind and body wrestle to drag each other down, the senses hang on for dear life.

The next morning Mom is up, showered, dressed, medicated and agreeable by 9:00 am. We meet with Judy. "I have to think of Lena," Judy says. "She's my resident. She's 95 years old and may not be up to taking care of her sister. We don't have situations like this, here. Our residents are higher functioning. They're not used to such episodes. But I'll leave it up to Lena," Judy suggests, feigning diplomacy.

Judy is a good administrator. She knows her residents. She understands who Lena is. She knows that Lena will have to side with her because Lena seeks the approval of authority. She likes to fit in and be liked. This is why Mom is making Lena so nervous. Lena needs to look good. All her life, Lena strove to fit in with the people who mattered. A child of immigrants, Lena was forced to quit school in the eighth grade to help support the family of thirteen. All her life, Lena felt cheated and embarrassed by her lack of education. She overcompensates by working hard and long, maintaining a serious and upstanding demeanor, and seeing things unromantically in black or white, with no time for shades of gray. Her siblings and parents always referred to Lena as "our lawyer" because of her steadfast decisions and unwavering mind. Now, Mom's behavior isn't looking good, and Lena is being asked to cast judgment.

"I have to agree with you, Judy. I'm getting too nervous," says Lena.

Lena sentences Mom back to Philadelphia. I sense her misgivings when we leave, but characteristically she sticks to her decision.

On the plane ride home, Mom says, "I never thought I'd be rejected by my own family. I really liked it there with Lena. What happened?" Mom never remembers her foul moods when she is not in one. Why remind her, and risk losing the blessing of a clear moment.

"You know how Lena is, Mom," I offer. "She always sucks up to authority. Besides, Judy didn't feel it was right for you. Don't worry Mom. We're going home now."

I try to sound comforting. But where's home? I don't know. I know I'm not taking her back to her room in assisted-living. It would be torture for us both, after the (mostly) warm and comforting feeling of being with Lena in Florida. Besides, I'm feeling solidarity with Mom against the forces that would exclude her. I want her to feel loved by her family and world. Mom is finishing off one of the Haagen-Dazs ice cream bars I purchased before boarding to ease the pain of rejection.

"Trace, I wish this plane ride would never end." I press my face into the hanging flab of Mom's thin arm beside me, mournful for the ample and muscular arm that was my haven as a child.

"Me too, Mom. Me too." I'm licking chocolate almond slivers from the corners of my mouth, my head rests on Mom's meager arm, and I'm grateful for the limbo of this moment.

A Brief Interlude

Family Mosaic

Spring, 1966

"IT'S CALLED A MOSAIC, BUB. YOU HANG IT ON THE WALL!" I raise my voice to say this because Bubbe Ida, my grandmother, is not wearing her hearing aid. My mother, rushing around as usual, forgot about inserting it when she helped her to dress this morning. Bubbe didn't remind her. She'd rather not be bothered with it. It rings when she forgets to turn it down for a phone call. She finds it clunky and uncomfortable in her ear. She wears it to please us. Today, I am not pleased.

I am ten years old and my mother has left me to Bubbe-sit. Bubbe-sitting is what we do to keep our grandmother busy. One of us, me or another grandchild stays at her house for a few hours to give her a younger child to focus on, in an effort to keep her from worrying about the mixed-up lives of her grown children. Bubbe had her first heart attack when she was, I'm told, a fat and energetic 75-year-old. Now she is 85, shrunken and slow moving. Flabby skin hangs from her arms that used to be thick with muscle. My cousins and I call them "chicken arms." I hope there's a cure for them before I'm old. My mother says that Bubbe needs us around to "monitor her weak heart". I think her heart is weak from worrying so much. My mother is helping my father handle the lunch trade at his South Philadelphia luncheonette, Abie's Hot Dogs. She took my youngest brother, Myles, with her. He is five and trails her every movement as she works behind the counter.

"Take milekh, Momele," Bubbe insists. My name is Tracy, but Bubbe calls me Momele or Tracele. "*Momele* means 'my little love,'" my mother says. Bubbe's quivering hands place a tall glass of cold milk to the right of my mosaic. Her eyes follow my fingers as I outline the vase, flowers, and butterfly with string. I fill pasted spaces with tiny pink, purple and white stones, each to its own color-coded section.

"No Bub, I gotta finish before my mother gets back." A fluorescent bulb lights from above the kitchen table where I work. The constant hum of the bulb competes for my attention with each measured tick...tick...tick... of the wall clock. It is all so loud, vibrating in my ears as I work. I feel like I'm at the center of a beating heart, like the one you can walk through at the Franklin Institute Science Museum. Every second in her small apartment is counted out to me. I notice every movement. My hands travel back and forth from stones to paste to the beat. Bubbe seems oblivious to everything but me.

"Finish, Tracele," she hovers and pushes the milk closer. "You work so hard." The air is close in Bubbe's dining room. I'm breathing in the smell of puffed wheat and milk from her breakfast. Fresh air makes her feel chilly, so no windows are open. I'd rather be here at night, especially on Friday nights when Bubbe makes dinner for our whole family. All my cousins come with my aunts and uncles, their voices drown out the clock, constant arrivals freshen the air, and the apartment smells sweet like cookies. My Aunt Minnie usually brings a Beatles cake with long strands of chocolate frosting hair running down the sides and thick chocolate bangs made from jimmies. I have five aunts— my mother's older sisters. Between them, they take care of Bubbe's needs. Aunt Jean lives with Bubbe, but works during the day. Aunt Lena lives down the street, but comes over to help her bathe and dress in the morning. Aunt Bess stops to visit during the day on her way to and from work. My mother runs the errands and takes her to the doctor. The other two live nearby and call frequently. Although my mother's four brothers live nearby, they don't come as often. The phone rings and I jump at the intrusion, so piercing even Bubbe can hear it. I am rescued from her warm breath on my neck as she clomps her black oxfords across the linoleum floor to answer the phone.

She holds the receiver with two hands, trapping the twisted chord between her right elbow and breast. Her breast runs the length of her forearm and she squeezes it to her chest as she speaks. She struggles to hear the caller. "Nu?" she sighs. Her head rotates side to side. "Tt, tt, tt, tt, tt," her tongue clicks the roof of her mouth to show how sorry she is. Bubbe has started worrying. "Come Yussele, I'll give you what I have." Her voice becomes softer. She grips the receiver like a vise to her rocking head. She still calls her children by their Jewish, childhood names.

That was her eldest son, my Uncle Joe, on the phone. He roams the Philadelphia streets drunk and singing, "Smile, 'though your heart is breaking...." He lives in a boarding house somewhere, but often sleeps in a cot in the basement of my father's store. I've seen the rats in that basement, and I've heard the story of his decline.

Forty years ago, Joe had a job, a wife and a tiny daughter. When his wife Rose died of the common cold, before the days of penicillin, he brought his three-year-old daughter, Lillian, home to Bubbe and Zayde Max, my grandfather. When Joe remarried, he didn't take his child with him. He left her with Bubbe and Zayde. This was fortunate because he was later struck in the head by the 50 trolley while crossing Fourth Street. "He got up and walked away but he was never the same," is how my aunts tell the story. Bubbe embraced his daughter Lillian as her own, although they had no extra money.

Zayde Max said, "We have ten children, we can have eleven."

Bubbe said, "We're rich in family."

Zayde Max died when I was two, but I know him from our home movies. He had a wide, toothless smile. He didn't like to wear his dentures. He liked to wiggle his ears and ham it up for the camera. He didn't need to speak English well to make people laugh. Zayde was an orthodox Jewish miller in Czarist Russia who traveled to America by boat in 1909. Bubbe and their five small children followed him months later when he sent the fare. They settled in Philadelphia, having five more babies.

"He kept us laughing to keep from crying," my aunts said. "He could never stay with any job or money-making venture without drinking up the profits. He had a hard time adjusting to America. Once, he got a job in a gun factory." My aunts would start giggling at the thought of it. Then one of them would blurt. "He almost shot his pecker off! That was the end of that job." When the children were small, he drove a horse and buggy selling rags, or the discarded coal and fruit that could be found by the train tracks.

"We were so poor," my Aunt Bessie told me, "that Lena used to hoist me up into the sitting railroad cars on Oregon Avenue, when no one was looking, and I'd fill a pillowcase with coal for the furnace, otherwise we'd have no heat in winter!"

When I asked Aunt Lena about this, her face turned red and she said, "We would never do such a thing. We were good children."

As soon as the older kids could watch the younger ones, Bubbe Ida began a hot dog business, parking a pushcart on the busy, market corner of Fourth and South Streets. She made her own pepper hash—a colorful mixed relish concoction from her Russian peasant background. She sold hot dogs with "the works" (mustard, onions, pepper hash and sauerkraut) with an orange drink for five cents. Her business was a success and in time my mother, the ninth of Bubbe's ten children would take over her station at the pushcart after school.

"Bubbe would go home and make dinner for the family," says my mom. She continues with, "…Once when I was in high school, my girlfriends walked by and saw me on South Street all hunched over, carrying buckets of hot water to drain the steam ovens into the sewer. I almost died from embarrassment. I looked like an old lady. But that never stopped me from helping my mother. I knew how hard she worked. And boy, was she proud of her business! She'd line up her coins in stacks on the kitchen table at night, nickels on nickels, dimes on dimes. On a good day, she could take in five dollars! At dusk, Zayde would clean up and push the cart to a garage. Then I would go home to do my homework. I got so bored standing at that pushcart all afternoon. I memorized the alphabet backwards! ZYXWVUTSRQPONMLKJIHG-FEDCBA, so there!" She points her finger at me and smiles when she recites that, which makes me feel like I should be able to do it too. But I've never been that bored.

"That pushcart kept our family from starving through the Great Depression and World War Two," Mom boasts. I can't imagine anyone starving with Bubbe around pushing food on them.

My mom was the top student in English at South Philadelphia High School for Girls. She was awarded a copy of *The Complete Works of William Shakespeare* at graduation. It stands on the shelf in our dining room. She always loved to write. Now she writes letters to the editor of Philadelphia's evening *Bulletin* when she's upset about current events. Or if she sees a play that she likes, she writes to congratulate the producer. She never went to college. She decided to work as a bookkeeper after high school, to support her aging parents. Now she keeps the books for my father's store and assists behind the counter.

Sixteen years ago, in 1950, Bubbe and Zayde as well as many of their children and extended family purchased new homes, all of them first-time homeowners, in a newly settled section of Northeast Philadelphia. Their home on 6727 Horrocks St. is where Zayde Max died, where Bubbe began to decline, and devote her days to worrying about her children. She makes dinner every Friday night for her entire extended family. We eat in shifts around her dining room table. My family lives two blocks away. That's why I'm always here Bubbe-sitting.

"Vays mere," Bubbe returns the phone to its cradle. "Claina kinda, claina tzuris. Groysa kinda, groysa tzuris." She rolls her 'r's and her eyes, and baby-steps back to me. I don't know much Yiddish but I can tell from the sound of her sighs that it means something like—small children, small problems, big children, big problems. Her head never stops its rotation back and forth. "Nu, Momele, drink your milekh." We are back to this. I accept her doting as one of my Bubbe-sitting duties. She can focus on me for a few hours. I know this makes her happy. But I am worried about missing my art class this afternoon.

"If my mother doesn't show up soon..." I grumble. Now, my head is rotating like Bubbe's. My mother arrives. She beams at me as she catches her breath.

"Well done!" she crows, seeing my artwork. "We'll hang that up on the kitchen wall! How about it, Trace?"

She puts her packages on the sofa, including Myles, who has been asleep, slung across her shoulder. She sits down on my chair at Bubbe's table and drinks my milk, dunking a stray animal cracker from her pocket. She doesn't stop to take off her heavy winter coat. The pockets are deep and fat, full of used Kleenex, half sticks of chewing gum, and snacks for Myles. I think about how warm that milk must be by now.

Bubbe tells Mom about Uncle Joe's phone call. She reports other news from within the family. Although we try to keep bad news from Bubbe to give her less to worry about, she always hears this. She's like a sponge, absorbing her children's problems. It's like she's trying to protect them from getting sick, losing their jobs, or fighting with each other by suffering for them.

"It's pretty good, huh?" I say to my mother and Bubbe. I point to my artwork, trying to lighten them up. I'm finally seeing the mosaic as a whole image on a wooden board, now that I'm done focusing on each section. It's kind of like our family—Bubbe and Zayde, their ten children, and their children's children—all sections to fill in and worry about.

But when Bubbe makes dinner, they come together and everybody's happy, even though they're really not. I'm thrilled that I have a finished creation to hang on the kitchen wall next to my older brother Lanse's woodcuts. Mom says maybe I'll be an artist when I grow up. She prompts me to pack up my paste, string, and leftover stones as it's time for my art class. She gathers her keys and a prescription to be dropped off, and places them in the pocketbook hanging from her left arm. There is a jar of Bubbe's homemade soup and a baggie filled with the boiled, tasteless chicken whose flavor was sacrificed for the soup. She puts this in a shopping bag hanging from her right arm. She picks up Myles, slings him across her shoulder, and then takes my mosaic in her plump, wide hands. We leave Bubbe alone again in her apartment, and begin our descent to the street. Somewhere between the third and fourth step down, either Myles or the chicken shifts. The delicate balance between her burden and my art is thrown off, as she grabs for the railing on her right. Wood and iron collide. Purple, pink and white stones cascade the steps filling the spaces of our path below.

"Oh no!" my mother and I shriek in chorus. Myles, aroused by the panic in our voices, begins sobbing and tries to break free. She clutches him tighter.

"Tt, tt, tt, tt, tt" Bubbe's head, rotating out of control, emerges from behind the screen door. "You worked so hard, tt, tt, tt, tt."

"Sweetheart, I'm so sorry, I'm so sorry..." My mother's repetition isn't helping.

"It's OK! I know you didn't mean to drop it." I start kicking at the stones to show her it's okay.

"Here Trace, take the chicken. Take the damn chicken!"

She's angry; not at me but at herself for carrying so much that she ended up dropping the artwork. Mom hands a part of her burden down to me, as the stones of my mosaic settle into the cracks in the sidewalk on Horrocks Street.

My House Is Your House

Spring, 2003

As soon as the plane touches ground, the cell phone resting on my thigh begins to vibrate. My stomach answers in waves of nausea. We are back in the land of decision-making. We remain seated for another half-hour, as the crew awaits an arrival gate assignment. I wish someone else would assign Mom to her next living arrangement. That would make my life easier in a way, but not really. I am choosing to remain at the helm. I respond to the buzzing cell phone. It's my brother Myles calling to commiserate.

"It's all I can think about since yesterday," he says. He had called the day before during the heat of the meeting with Judy and Lena. I had kept him on the line so he could overhear the proceedings. He heard Judy asking Mom what she wanted, and Mom saying she wanted to stay with Lena. Myles was moved by my appeals to Judy to give Mom another chance, stunned by her refusal, and by Lena's agreement with Judy. Listening in has made him sympathetic to my struggle.

"What am I going to do, Myles?" I whisper into the phone, looking to my right at Mom to see if she is paying attention. "I can't take her back to her room at The Protestant Home, not after Florida. She liked Florida!"

"Apparently, Florida didn't like her," he quips.

"I mean, at first. She liked the food, and Lena was good company. If only she hadn't…" I stop myself before getting lost in "if onlys."

"Why don't you take her home with you?" Myles suggests. "You work at home, during the week anyway, and I can take her on weekends."

"Really! That might work."

I'm encouraged by this hint of support. Finally, someone in my vicinity is offering to share the load. Of course, did I ever ask for help? Why do I always wait for help to be offered? I never learned to ask. He says he'll take her on weekends! Hallelujah! I'm actually smiling as I say goodbye. I turn off my cell phone and sink back into my seat. Mom is dozing beside me. I shut my eyes and let my thoughts take over, while the flight crew still waits for a gate. I think about how different my situation might be, had I sisters. My mother's five, as well as her niece Lily were always around, helping each other–dropping off a jar of soup after work, picking up my favorite brownies from the bakery, lending and borrowing cars and clothes. When Mom and Dad took a vacation, Aunt Bess would stop by to make us oatmeal in the morning before school.

Now, I am alone in this. Mom's family is gone except for Aunt Lena, and that option has just evaporated. Mom used to say, "My only regret, Trace, is that I couldn't give you sisters." She treasured hers. Instead, she gave me brothers, who leave the job to me. Perhaps it's a learned habit, passed down from the older generation. I don't remember my uncles being so involved with my grandmother's care. It was never expected of them, so how could they expect it of themselves? This is what we witnessed as children, and perhaps it's why I have a hard time asking for help from my brothers. Tony calls it my "God complex." I think I can do it all–that I'm superhuman. He is supportive, but not too involved, either. I wonder if I'd had a female partner, would that make it easier? Women feel compelled to seek solutions for each other, extending themselves emotionally and physically. Or perhaps if I'd never married, never had a child. I'd move back in with my mother and stay with her until the end. I know it's not necessarily what I'd wanted, but certainly decisions would be simpler. Such is the state of my mind—grasping at "if onlys" once again.

The reality of the situation is that I am best suited for this job, which is why my mother initially gave me the power of attorney. Recalling her trust now gives me confidence. The challenge recharges me. Unlike a hired caregiver, I know who she is beneath the illness. I will not define her by it. And if I am the one who cares for her, I will never feel guilty about how she is cared for. I will simply care for my mother as lovingly as she has cared for me, in the comfort of my own home. I turn in my seat toward Mom. "We're going home, Mom!" I say. "I'm excited about it. My house is your house. Don't argue with me."

This time, she doesn't argue. In the past she has said, "Just put me somewhere. I don't want to be a burden." But now, Mom seems relieved by my decision and determined to help me make this work. Her eyes are brighter. She looks hopeful and a little more confident. Perhaps she overheard my conversation with Myles–how we are working together toward a solution. Perhaps she's proud of us. Maybe the silver lining in all this is that it's bringing her children together. Perhaps she realizes that I need to take care of her myself. She will come to my house because it is the best solution for me now. Our bond has grown stronger since making this trip. She knows the distance I will go to make her happy, and she realizes that she still has the capacity to experience a little happiness. Myles, by extending himself, has helped us off the plane and into the next phase of this journey. The plane glides up to the gate, and we make our way up the aisle and down the ramp. Mom is walking erect, just holding onto my arm. We are met with a wheelchair at the end of the ramp, and Mom settles in. I pick up the pace and gather our luggage. Then, I call Tony.

"I'm bringing my mother home to live with us," I announce. "I can't take her back to assisted living. I just can't. She seems almost normal, now. Florida was good for her, in a way. I want to keep this going as long as I can. Trust me on this." It is not posed as a question. My decision has been made. I don't know if this is the best decision for our marriage, but I do know that I can make no other choice.

"I hope you know what you're doing," is all he says. He sounds doubtful, even threatening.

"I know what I'm doing. See you soon." I put my efforts into normalcy—a kind of welcoming party. "We'll stop and bring home Chinese food for dinner." I am lighter now that I'm moving into familiar territory. I'm nervous about Tony's reaction, but he doesn't try to change my mind. I'm sure I sound relieved, even hopeful. And when I relax, so does my family. I know I can handle this job. It feels dharmic, as the Hindus refer to a well-suited task. I feel more in control of my demented world than I have in a while. I know I can depend on myself. I can manage my mother, my daughter, our marriage and photography business all under one roof. And when all needs are met, I will lie in bed and read, The *Grapes of Wrath*, for sustenance. At least we'll all have a roof above us. I call in the dinner order and bring it home, along with Mom. Amity lights on me, clinging to me with constant hugs. Later, I will hear from her kindergarten teacher that she was uncharacteristically sullen while I was gone. She is fine with sharing me, so long as I stay put. She welcomes her demented grandmother with attentive chatter. My daughter needs me to be home, regardless of whom else I carry. Tony is watchful and willing to see where this will lead, so long as I again assume the reins of our household. He hugs us both but I feel in his thin frame that he is holding something back. He has always had a good relationship with my mother and shares my desire to do what's right by her. But Mom's anxiety (and mine) weighs him down. It looks to me as if he'd like to escape. After all, he has just spent practically a week as a single parent, and now I'm adding a sick mother-in-law to the mix. He retreats into our garage/business office, as soon as he can. We say little to each other.

Tony is the youngest of five sons from an old Philadelphia Main Line family. Until he was twelve, the family had full-time, household help, including Blanche, the nanny who practically raised him. When we discuss our families and how we came of age, we find that despite our socio-economic and cultural differences, there are more similarities between us than not. For example, our parents' laissez faire attitude toward child rearing. There weren't many rules or expectations—just "stay out of trouble," which we both, in families with many children interpreted as—keep your mischievous activities under the radar. Neither of us caused too much trouble for our parents because we never let on what we were doing, and they never asked. But there was a distinct difference between our families that Tony learned to love. Back in the late 1980s when my aunts were alive, I would bring Tony to Aunt Jean's apartment for dinner on Friday nights. Aunt Jean lived in the apartment that had been Bubbe Ida's, and she carried on the tradition that Bubbe Ida started. The crowd of family and friends already seated at the dining room table would greet us with wild applause as we walked in. In fact, this is how they greeted all guests, but for Tony, raised in a more formal, staid environment, it was too much expressed emotion. He would have to lie down in a back bedroom at first to regain his composure. He just wasn't used to all the attention. Then when he sat down at the table, my aunts would crowd around filling his plate for him. "Look how thin he is. Watch how he sucks the marrow out of the chicken bones," Bessie would announce to the crowd. She developed a running commentary about Tony's eating habits. It wasn't derogatory; he was just a curiousity. When he chose to exclude wheat in his diet and informed my aunts that he couldn't eat the pasta in the traditional kasha and bowtie dish, they presented him with "Tony's kasha" without the bowties—a large mound of browned buckwheat groats growing larger every time he feigned enthusiasm. He learned to love the benign, somewhat smothering display of affection. Tony— with his boyish, "goyishe" good looks and dry humor, and Bessie with her unfiltered, un-self-conscious comments, developed an ongoing, flirtatious rapport. I often thought that one of the reasons he wanted to marry me was because of what he received at those dinners—a warmth he never truly felt from his family of origin. But now I'm asking him to accept something new—a responsibility I feel that comes along with the unconditional love we were fed. And although I think he appreciates how I feel, I don't think he is made for this struggle. Still I know what I must do and for now, he will have to accept it.

We unpack the Chinese food and eat from cartons at the dining room table. We relax into the familiar aromas of food and family. With faces glowing from Florida sunshine, Mom and I present Amity and Tony with the sweet souvenirs of our journey—sugarcoated orange jellies and chocolate coconut patties. Mom raises her cup of Chinese tea and toasts, "If I could just hold onto this moment, this night with my family." She beams as she says this, again the toastmistress, sitting erect and holding her cup out to each one of us. Her fist, so tight around the cup that her hand shakes, reveals her grasp on what she has to lose and her willingness to put up a fight. I sip strong tea from one of the Franciscan patterned china cups that came from my mother's house, savoring each astringent mouthful before swallowing.

Later, we call Lena to tell her we've arrived safely. Mom and Lena speak amicably about their time together. "It's nice to go away and it's nice to come home," Mom says, just as she always used to when returning from a trip. I'm glad they've had one last reunion in person, and glad that we are home. As hopeful as things seem right now for Mom, I'm glad that Lena will not have to witness the inevitable progression of her sister's end-of-life nightmare. Lena sounds relieved. I think she needs to hear that Mom is happy to assuage her guilt. I can sense that she is deeply disappointed that they won't be living together and conflicted about her decision, but ultimately falls back on her stoic pragmatism, developed over a lifetime of facing disappointment head-on. "I can't manage her and Judy agrees, period."

I imagine that Lena tells herself this, deferring to authority and moving on, as she did for over fifty years of marriage to Uncle Harry. But Lena doesn't seem to want to hang up the phone. It feels like she's waiting for something from

Mom. Lena needs to hear from Mom that she is forgiven. In fact, she needs Mom's approval. And Mom, the obedient and respectful younger sister complies.

"I'm kissing you through the phone, Lena dear," Mom emotes before closing. Lena squeals in delight and hangs up. Then Mom goes into the bathroom and has the bowel movement she's been anticipating all week.

Crossing Over

Early Summer, 2003

My kitchen has become the hub of our lives. From its island nucleus with a stained and battered stovetop and crowded counter, our new lifestyle emerges. Mom's medications compete for space and priority with our vitamins, Chinese herbs and Amity's snacks. The wholesome beans, rice, and whole grains to which my husband and daughter have been accustomed, sit languishing on the shelf as I whip up the dinners of my youth. Strawberries and sour cream, cherry blintzes, noodles and cottage cheese...

"We're having dairy tonight," I announce, just as Mom did when I was a child at home. Platter after over-flowing platter of dairy-rich, carbohydrate-heavy delicacies cover the dining room table. Mom devours the familiar flavors. She allows me to mother her. She cleans her plate and asks for seconds.

"Boy do I love Jewish food!" Tony announces to his friends and family. He's thrilled with this part of our altered lives. It's exotic to him. He was raised on a diet of creamed chipped beef on toast and lamb with mint jelly. But the best part for Tony and Amity is having home-cooked meals on the table at regular hours, without me leaving to help Mom either physically or emotionally in response to her lack of care. Mom is enjoying her stay with us, and we enjoy caring for her. The Protestant Home nightmare is over. Florida was a brief respite. We've settled into a semblance of everyday life. We're grateful for this lack of drama. When Mom shows a small but somewhat upbeat response to my efforts, I am thrilled. I have adjusted my expectations and don't expect her to be normal, just okay and agreeable. Catering to her gives me another child to mother. I like having control over her environment. I keep her busy with small chores around the house and away from the loneliness that almost destroyed her. I know that future loss is inevitable, but I'm content not to deal with that, until I have to. We've reached a plateau. It's emotionally restful, although I hardly rest. It's early June, and Mom seems better than she was last December. I feel I'm being given the gift of time. For however long this lasts, we'll make the most of it. The guest room is now "Bubbe's room," complete with private bath modified with a shower handle to accommodate her increasing needs. We bring in the bureau from her bedroom at home and cover the top with framed pictures of family. The four-poster bed, originally Tony's parents' and the fine-art photography on the walls is familiar to her as is my house, so the transition is easy under the circumstances. This has become her home. When Mom hears Amity talk about school, she asks, "When am I going to school?" She has settled into being my other child.

"I'll find you one, Mom," I promise. This prompts me to find the Main Line Adult Day Center, or "Bubbe's school," as we call it, held in a nearby church. Mom is actually content to spend her weekdays there while I work, although she admits she is frightened that I might forget to pick her up. I collect her after picking up Amity and her friends from school. The "school for old people" is a source of fascination to Amity, Jared, and Evan (the two boys who live next door).

"What do they do there all day?" Evan, the oldest and most curious asks. "They already learned to read and write, and probably know their geography."

"They learn how to be old," is all I can think to say. The kids breathe fresh energy into the closed-in spaces of a worn-out building. Their quick race down the halls does more for the slumping, disassociated "students" than all the fish tanks and guinea-pig cages on the sidelines. We are allowed to take their guinea pigs home for the weekend, as long as we promise to come back with them. We all ride home together discussing the day, guinea pigs wheeking in the background.

Mom seems content to listen. Despite never getting to sit down to a meal, rarely sleeping or taking the time to wash my hair, I am noticeably happier with this arrangement. I am no longer managing long-distance caregivers for better or worse. I am the hands-on caregiver, and I satisfy my own expectations. I'm the nurse, the cook, the social worker and the psychologist, and I'm on top of it all. No medication is overlooked or mismanaged. No more frantic phone calls or disappointing responses. Again, life is in my control and I keep it on track. Still, I'm reading *American Pastoral* by Philip Roth, and waiting for my new, carefully crafted home life to go horribly awry. Both Amity and Bubbe have their rituals in the car each morning, while I drive them to school. My 83-year-old, demented mother sitting in front, applies a perfect line of lipstick without a mirror, breaks a stick of gum in half, pops it into her mouth and passes the other half, along with the lipstick, to six-year-old Amity in the back seat.

"How about it, Am?" Mom throws the gum and orange lipstick over her right shoulder and Amity catches.

"Thanks, Bubbe." Amity is not so skilled at the application but she purses her lips together afterwards just like Bubbe. I watch Mom drawing from an ingrained routine to face the public, and Amity behind her, happily learning to present her public face. This ritual sustains us all. Their shared moment keeps Amity agreeable to sharing so much of me with her grandmother. Mom is gaining weight. She loves the Jewish comfort food. She never leaves the dinner table without her last course— three scoops of Breyer's vanilla ice cream and a handful of pretzels. Regardless of mental or emotional status, she always welcomes dessert. And no matter how much I eat to keep her company, my five-foot frame keeps melting. I'm down to ninety pounds.

"Are you ready for bed, Mom?" I call from the kitchen as I finish washing dishes, leaving them to air dry until morning. Mom pushes herself away from the table and looks up at me. Her childlike expression mixes comfort and fear.

"I'm scared but you'll help me." Ascending the steps to her bedroom is an arduous journey, taken earlier and earlier into the evenings. The fear of falling drains her energy for the climb. She grips the rail with her left hand and my waist with her strained, quivering right. Her clutch, and the desperate crook of her boney right arm around my thinning middle, both enslave and support me. We are almost posed photographically, as we scale the steps. Our changing bodies and shared fortitude stand up to her fears. And I feel so necessary. I have thought about installing a chair-elevator by the stairway for Mom, but they are expensive and Tony is against doing anything that might permanently alter our home. I'm not sure if a stair lift would, but I cross this off my list.

Sometimes Mom awakens in the middle of the night, afraid and calling for help. I lie awake, alert to these appeals, because I don't want her to disturb Amity. Sometimes I lie in bed with Mom and fall asleep.

"Mom? Mom!" Amity stands at the doorway to Bubbe's room. She has awakened, wandered into my room, and not found me in bed. "Why are you sleeping with Bubbe?" Her tone is accusatory.

"Did you hear her calling out? Did she wake you up, honey?" I don't directly answer Amity's question, nor does she answer mine. I take her hand and we go back into my bed until morning. Tony avoids the entire rotation by holing up in another bedroom, surrounded by an arsenal of white-noise machines. This four-bedroom house that we, at one time imagined filling with children, has finally come in handy. Mom's morning descent is usually accomplished on her bottom. She bumps down step-by-step with an allowance for recovery time between each jolt. We move like this for three-quarters of a year—from winter through spring to summer. My resolve remains to accommodate all losses for as long as possible, despite each step downward in Mom's ability to sustain the happy moments.

Amity is graduating from kindergarten, and the house is buzzing with talk of new clothes and shoes. Mom, always the party-girl, perks up on the morning of the big event. She still loves a celebration. "Would you like to attend Amity's graduation ceremony, Mom? They call it, 'Crossing Over.'" This last-minute invitation is deliberate. I don't usually plan things ahead of time for Mom. Everything depends on her mood.

"Well, of course I would." She swells with grandmotherly pride.

On the uneven ground of the school's outdoor theater, Mom struggles with her walker and her inner turmoil. She looks miserable, wearing her permanent scowl and yet determined with a death grip on the handles of her walker, to shove it through the grassy patch leading to the rows of benches on a decline, surrounding the stage. With the help of one of my friends, present to witness Amity's assent, Mom settles onto a wobbly bench. Meanwhile, I am busy unloading photo equipment from the car. On stage, in the middle, is a freestanding, wooden, ceremonial bridge that the school keeps tucked away all year just for this event. The speeches begin and the graduates' names are called. On cue, hand in hand with a sixth-grade escort, Amity crosses over—skipping across the wooden, ceremonial bridge from kindergarten to the first grade.

"That was beautiful. She's so adorable," Mom stage whispers to me from her seat on the second row, aisle.

I kneel in front to take pictures from a wide angle making use of my wedding photography equipment for this occasion. Through my camera I see Tony wandering the periphery capturing the light with a long lens and a narrow depth of field, momentarily throwing the background out of focus. As I watch Amity scale the upward slope, stop to wave, and then scuttle down the decline of the "Bridge to Elementary," I wish I could say that I am enjoying the moment. Instead, I'm thinking about the upward struggle of the last year, and the unstoppable downward course of Mom's future. This crest will be brief. But I've been a professional photographer for almost twenty years and instinct tells me to freeze this clichéd image—the pose on the mount, the proud wave to family and friends, one foot already turned toward the future, as if we could just stay right here forever. Later, I will glimpse at a 4x6 print of this moment to finally enjoy it—a brief escape from the ravages of time.

I sit beside Mom at the luncheon, afterwards. She is becoming increasingly messy and needs help to eat in public. I keep blotting her fresh stains with a cloth napkin dipped in drinking water. I notice some of the other parents watching me. Most of them are younger than me, and I imagine they have youthful, supportive parents. I can feel how foreign this seems to them. However, when they glance and look away, I'm not embarrassed. I'm determined, especially in public. I want Mom to remain involved. Meanwhile, Amity runs off with her friends after taking a few solid bites of her celebratory lunch.

"Delicious food and great company! Right Mom?" I recruit the optimistic spirit of her past to brighten up her present. I want to believe that joyful events will stave off Mom's dementia, but time is not on her side.

Amity begins day camp, which is conveniently located next door to Mom's day care. Our morning routine remains the same. I'm looking forward to Parents' Day at camp to witness Amity's newly acquired swim skills. These designated moments of parenthood take on greater import for me as I struggle to balance Mom's care with the rest of my life. I am determined not to cheat anyone.

There is a new and wholly unexpected dimension to my caregiving duties, and I do mean duties. Mom's bowels often become impacted, or at least her butt muscles forget how to work. At any rate, she frequently finds herself in a "half-way there" position and calls out to me from the toilet: "I can't finish, Trace. My BM is stuck! Can't you help me? I can't go anywhere like this. Please, Trace..."

So now I'm learning about proctology, as my gloved fingers explore places most people have never been. I release hardened balls of feces, which feel like the coal in a bar-b-que, but are caked in layers of aging, unmoved, undigested dinner– little atoms crammed into a tight space. I free the hardened masses, allowing for fresher, softer, more pliable remnants to scurry through her now unblocked passage. "I feel great, Trace! Where are we going, today?" Mom finishes up, while I remove my gloves and wash and re-wash my hands about fifteen times with warm water and soap. I dry and apply hand sanitizer up and down my arms. I take out the trash, freshen the air in the bathroom, and wash my hands a couple of times more. After all evidence of human stain is removed from the house, we're good to go.

Myles calls after one of these sessions, and I fill him in on the messy details of caregiving, bragging about my macho, tough-girl endeavor and emphasizing the distance one must go in order to care for our mother. It's another competition between us, which I feel compelled to let him know I have won. (Ha! Who else would or could do this? Only me! You guys just don't have what it takes.) Unfortunately, this wins me the battle but loses the war. After my graphic description of daughterly devotion, Myles never takes Mom home with him for the weekend. And I don't push him to do it. I just hire a weekend caregiver service for when I'm working.

While Tony and I are at work photographing brides on Saturdays and Sundays, the house is full of people. Amity and her babysitter, and Mom and her caregiver compete for space. To keep the couples from clashing, I pre-plan field trips for Amity and her sitter–to the park, to the movies, the Philadelphia Zoo, the Franklin Institute Science Museum—anything for a diversion. Mom is not as agreeable with the hired help as she is with me. One Saturday while I'm working, the new (they don't last long) and very frustrated caregiver calls.

"Your mother won't do anything I ask. She's yelling at me! She won't even use the towel I hand her!"

"Well, just let her be for a while," I suggest. I return to my task of photographing a jam-packed ballroom full of drunken people who don't notice my distraction. I'm wondering if this new person will bail on me today, and how long it will be until all hell breaks loose in our household. How long till I can't find a patient enough caregiver? How long till Mom, Amity and Tony each need more attention than I can give them?

But when I get home, I see the unused hand towel and understand immediately what happened. It had been a guest towel, hanging only for show in the bathroom of my parents' house for 50 years. We were not allowed to use it–a black towel, monogrammed aKs in pink to match the tile–a gift for the new house in 1950. In my house, it's just one among the mix of fraying hand-me-downs. But Mom follows the 50-year-old rule: "We do not use that towel!" These kinds of small misunderstandings must happen all the time in nursing homes, I realize, because often people are placed there devoid of a past. I swear that no matter what the future brings, I'll be there to share Mom's story. Meanwhile on weekends, Amity enjoys the doting attentions of two people—her babysitter and Bubbe's caregiver. What a relief it must be for a person who's used to dealing with the aged to witness the energy of youth. But when Amity's energy collides with Bubbe's afternoon nap on the living room sofa, Bubbe awakens agitated, her eyes bulge, she balls her fists and screams, "Let me die! Let me die!" Amity retreats to the dining room, cowering under the table, palms pressed against her ears.

"When is Bubbe going home?" Amity asks.

"We're helping her feel better," I answer indirectly, still optimistic that I can control Mom's outbursts, or at least keep Amity away from them. I'm grateful for the open-door policy we have with our next-door-neighbors. Amity has a safe-haven there, when necessary. Also, Amity begins Hebrew School on Sunday mornings—convenient for getting her out of the house on a day that Mom is home from adult day care. I become finely attuned to Mom's changes. I cure her life-long problem with constipation by altering her diet. I can only do this because her mind is no longer involved. She no longer thinks about her constipation, her need for laxatives, or her food choices. She simply eats what she is served.

One morning she awakens and is unable to insert her own dentures. Up until now, having me insert her teeth would have been mortifying to her. This is her very last life-skill held onto with a grip stronger than Dentu-Crème. But she must relinquish even this. I'm not very good at handling dislocated teeth, and not just because of my lack of experience. The realization of what this means for her, paralyzes me. With this change, she surrenders her pride, dignity, and most remnants of her former personality. She freezes, becoming robotic while I do this, which doesn't help.

At breakfast, we notice that she is holding her spoon backwards and missing her mouth completely, as oatmeal drops into her lap. I'm reminded of "Backwards Day" at camp when I was a kid. We did this intentionally. I stop and stare at this new person in front of me. This is not intentional. It's taking me a few minutes to comprehend that this is what's called, "a change in mental status." Meanwhile, Mom arises from her chair, takes a few steps, then trips and hits her head on the wooden coffee table in the living room.

"Get away from me!" she screams at Tony who tries to help her. She won't allow us to pick her up off the floor. I realize that she must have suffered another mini-stroke during the night. We call an ambulance. Amity, Evan and Jared watch as paramedics carry Bubbe out of the house and load her into an emergency medical vehicle. She looks helpless and immediately remorseful, as if she were a bad child.

"Don't send me to the hospital, Trace," she says, looking directly at me as she leaves. I follow the van with my car and spend the day at the hospital with Mom, undergoing tests. After a few stabilizing days in the hospital, including several times of complete remission where her spirit reappears and then fades, she is moved to a convalescent home nearby for rehabilitation. Upon arrival, she bites her intake nurse and is declared "combative." She is settled into the "Dementia Unit."

This turns out to be a nicer room, more like a studio apartment with two beds in an L-shape, but at a distance from each other, not like a hospital room at all. It comes with an agreeable, although clueless, demented roommate with a deep, gravelly voice, probably the result of a life-long smoking habit. Mom remarks, "She sounds like our Jean," and I agree it's a comforting approximation of Aunt Jean's voice, even though her words make no sense.

Mom gets good attention from personable caregivers and I get a break. She's only a half-mile from my house but in her own space, with a little extra help. And she receives physical therapy. I often work out with her at the afternoon therapy sessions. As usual she thrives on the attention and activity. She comes home to stay, a couple of weeks later, and soon we are back on our routine. Mom is glad to be home and although everything is harder, her spirit continues to re-surface again at times–grateful and loving. When I mention this phenomenon to a visiting nurse, she smiles in recognition.

"We call those moments— blessings," She winks at me.

One summer night, Tony experiences a "blessing" first hand when he arrives home from photographing a wedding before I do. The next morning, he tells me about it. "So I tell the babysitter and caregiver they can go home, since Amity and Bubbe are both asleep. Then I hear your mom calling out for help. I go up to her room and she says she needs to go to the bathroom. I help her out of bed, and she clenches my wrists in a death grip as I practically drag her across the room to the bathroom. She keeps saying, 'I'm not gonna make it. I'm not gonna make it'. But she does. I wait for her to finish so I can help her back to the bed. Her upper torso is slumped in front of her as she sits on the toilet; it looks like her head will hit the floor any minute, like she has no muscle tone keeping her up. When I kneel to help pull up her Depends, she looks up at me, directly into my eyes in a way she hasn't since she's been sick. Her eyes are clear, compassionate, and she recognizes me. It's like her old self, good old upbeat Sylvie is visiting for a second. 'You're doing the right thing!' she says. She keeps nodding 'Yes' as she stares at me and she gives me a kind of resigned smile. Then she says, 'I'm proud of you, Tone. You're great!' At this point, I'm crying and I think she is too. But when I go to help her up, she struggles with me and pushes me away. She's totally gone by the time I get her back to the bed." I'm glad that Tony had one more real moment with Mom. And I'm glad that Mom took that moment to thank him.

Parents' Day arrives at Amity's camp. My plan is to take Mom to her school, then head straight to camp with Amity. Only, Mom won't get out of bed. After all the golden days of cooperative cohabitation, this is the day she drops the ball. "Get up, Mom, time to get dressed for school," I announce as usual, but now to no response. "Up time!" I say. This is a familiar phrase from my childhood: "Wake me when it's up time!" my brother Myles would say as a toddler. I try to invoke our family's lexicon, and the sweetness associated with the past. But this time my attempt to conjure a warm feeling doesn't elicit a response. Mom's body lies rigid in the bed, wrapped in a sheet. "Mom?" I brace myself and pull at her cover.

"What!" she barks.

"Time to go to school, remember?"

"Shut up!" The phrase rises like mucus in her throat. "Go to hell!" she spits. I wipe my face.

"Mom, if you don't get up, we won't be able to live together anymore. Remember?" I plead. She hisses and growls, like a threatened feral cat. The anger in her eyes orphans me. I know that if this continues, I might become just as abusive to her. My mother is gone. And yet this rage is somehow familiar. It's a member of our family, always there and never acknowledged. She is oozing years of frustration, of never being able to say, "I feel lousy." This illness is giving her something she'd never had—the freedom to complain.

"Aaaaaaaaaaahhhhhhhhhhhheeeeeeeee!! I want to die!!!!" She screeches through octaves she never sang. "Aaaaaaaaaaahhhhhhhhhheeeeeee!!!!! Let me die!!!!" Mom keens. She is grieving for her life, wailing for death. *I'm sick, damaged, and I have the right to scream.* It feels to me like some logical part of her brain is trying to cut through all the crap and reach out to me. Like she's trying to say to me, *I'll show you my terror, my fear, the hell of having to be dead and still in this body. Look at it with me. Acknowledge my anger and the truth of this situation. Don't make it any better than it is. Who you kiddin'? Just get me outta' here!* I feel threatened by her shrieks and the unsaid words beneath them. I feel like our past, all the happy memories and the optimism that was our family's approach to life is being threatened and beaten down by this illness. I feel like her screams are highlighting the anger and unspoken resentments that she never before acknowledged, and that I never presented to her. It just wasn't our way. And is this what happens when you turn away from the troubling things throughout life? Do your unspoken feelings come to haunt you in the end? If that's the case, I'm next in line for this illness.

The sheets are soaked, and her body, heavy with home cooking, is dead weight on the bed. The room smells like all the nursing homes I'd ever held my nose in. I flash back in memory to Mom's casual reference when she first recognized her growing depression and looming incontinence. "Wait. Soon, I'll start to smell," she sighed in knowledge and surrender.

I leave her there and drive Amity to camp. I still have an hour before I need to be poolside. I return home to find Mom in the same position, the bed saturated and stinking, her body unmoved. I manage to roll her, to clean beneath, and change the sheets. She responds by peeing on every clean sheet as I replace it. Then she grabs my hand and bites it.

"God damn it, Mom! That hurt!" I'm not thinking, I'm swinging my fist at her as hard as I can, but not connecting. Falling backwards, I begin to sob. "Ma, why? God damn you, WHY? WHAT THE FUCK IS WRONG WITH YOU?"

I go into the bathroom to wrap my bleeding palm in toilet paper. Why is this happening? Things were going so well. Why is it every time I solve one problem, a new one presents? And where's our big, warm, loving family? If only someone else could step in for me now. Why am I here alone carrying the weight of her torpid soul? It isn't the first time I've wanted to smack her. I know we're moving into dangerous territory. I know she is testing me.

Hit me back! Do something! How much will you take before you finally realize you can't stop this! Can we just quit this charade and bring on the inevitable? You can't save my life! How can you be so naïve?

My normal, practical mother's mind is speaking inside my head and I'm hearing that word again. Am I still so naïve? I pick up the phone, call around, and find the same bed available at the nearby convalescent home where she had been somewhat comfortable after her last stroke. In fact, she'll have the same demented, gravelly-voiced roommate. She listens immobile and without protest as I arrange for an ambulance to come for her in the afternoon. They'll lift her out of this stinking hellhole.

I leave her at home and drive back to Amity's camp for Parents' Day. Amity waits in the water, groping at the side of the pool's deep end. Finally, it's her turn. I watch her propel her shivering body with a quick thrust of her feet against the wall. She arches her back and trusts the water to support her glide. Our eyes meet and she smiles as she back-floats away from me. I give her the thumbs up and meet her with a beach towel as she climbs out of the water.

"I love you, Sweetheart. You're great!" I whisper, hugging her with the towel, and absorbing her shivers. Buoyed by Amity's success, I drive home from the pool determined to go forward with a new plan for Mom. Now, it will be more productive to assist her dying. It breaks my heart to admit that this part of our lives is over.

"Hi Trace. Here, help me get dressed," Mom greets me. She's sitting up in bed. Her legs hang over the side. We accomplish the morning routine, bump down the steps, and enjoy a nice, leisurely lunch. Now that she's moving, I cancel the ambulance. I can drive her, myself.

"Trace, don't take me back there," she says, as I help her to the car. She touches my cheek with the back of her hand, but it does not feel sincere. In all our life together, this has never been her way of expressing affection. This feels like she is play-acting. I'm being conned by a naughty child. I think of Patty McCormick in *The Bad Seed*. "I've been bad, but I'll be good, Mummy." I think she knows it is time for a nursing home. I know she doesn't want to put me through this morning's trial ever again. And she knows she will, if she stays on with me. But there is a part of her that has to try, however poorly acted. It feels to me like she's watching herself from a distance, going through the motions to put this period to rest. Still, I'm feeling like shit. What am I supposed to do now? Cancel the plan and go through this hell again tomorrow? I'm fed up and determined to regain control of my life. I feel manipulated, taken advantage of. I have become her emotional doormat and I must put a stop to it. I cry and drive her to the nursing home where she is promptly placed in a wheelchair and left alone. She slumps down into it and stares at her lap. I run off to retrieve Amity from camp.

"Where's Bubbe?" Amity stands rigid at the car door scanning the front and back seats before climbing in.

"I took her back to the nursing home where she was before."

"Good!" She climbs into the car seat and allows her body to go limp. I realize that Amity has spent her day in fear of coming home. Now she rips into her bag of popcorn rice cakes, stuffs her mouth full, and mindlessly chews. Her vacant eyes stare into a self-soothing space, as I drive the two of us home. Meanwhile I've developed a bad head cold and for the first time in months, I choose to lounge on our sunny back patio and indulge my exhaustion.

"Tracy, I'm hungry!" Four-year-old Jared from next-door, wanders over and greets me as usual. But today, I don't jump up to feed him.

"I'm tired, Jared. Help yourself. There are lots of snacks." Jared gives me a sidelong glance. His brow furrows.

He looks worried. This behavior is uncharacteristic of me. But we are all discovering limits. He returns from the kitchen with a rice cake for each of us.

Later we visit Bubbe, stopping along the way to bring her chocolate water ice and soft pretzels. She is quiet and receptive. My surrender of primary care for Mom gives me time to think—to obsess, about what I have done. I remember when I took Mom to Florida, Amity's kindergarten teacher, Mrs. Herron, mentioned Amity's distress at my absence. She said, "If you have to choose between your daughter and your mother, you must choose your daughter. She needs you more at this point. Your mother has already lived her life."

At that time, I thought I could choose both, and enhance each of their lives with the presence of the other. Whether I succeeded at that, I really don't know. In a way, Amity has won this battle, which doesn't make me feel any better. In fact, I will keep trying to compensate Mom—keep trying to make her happy. Our summer evenings are now spent slurping water ice together, all three of us, and sometimes Jared, on the patio of the nursing home.

A Day At The Beach

Late August, 2003

The dog days of summer are upon us, and I crave the ocean. Although Mom is in the "Dementia Unit" of a nursing home, she still looks forward to my visits. I often take her out for dinner or ice cream, so I can't take a vacation. But I can manage a long day at the beach with my husband and daughter. On a sweltering Thursday in late August, I plan a road trip for the following Sunday to Ocean City, New Jersey, some 60 miles away. We will meet friends on the beach, have dinner and a stroll on the boardwalk, and then come home. I will almost feel normal again.

On Thursday evening, as we sip iced tea on the shady patio of the nursing home, I tell Mom that I will bring her to my house for a bar-b-que on Saturday afternoon. "We'll grill hot dogs, roast corn on the cob and enjoy cold watermelon. In the good ol' summertime..." I sing to her. "Let's enjoy the summer while we have it, Mom. How's that sound?"

"Fine," she murmurs. Promising her a sunny Saturday bar-b-que, allows me to feel okay about taking off on Sunday. But I'm never quite okay, I never feel calm, I'm always in crisis mode. I feel that she's depending on me for life itself. It's my energy that gives her any life at all. It's miserable to see my mother so depressed and unhappy. It's unfair that this is her fate, and I can do nothing about it. I still can't accept that.

When Cousin Sybil (our Denny's wife) witnessed my extreme efforts to transport and include Mom at a recent family gathering, she commented, "You're in denial, Tracy." I resented that. I hate that people are saying, "Poor Tracy." I don't feel poor. I feel determined. I try to look as though nothing is wrong. Whatever new loss presents, I scurry to compensate. And when Mom has "a good day," when all circuits in her brain are suddenly firing, I rejoice and take this as justification to keep pushing, to keep pretending that everything is okay. But on Friday, Tony throws a snag in my plans. He suggests that we sleep at a seaside hotel on Saturday night. Amity and I can awaken early on Sunday and go bike riding, and he will catch up on his sleep. Everyone will be happy—everyone except Mom. I love the idea of sleeping over. Ordinarily, I would have suggested it myself. But now I feel split between the needs of my mother and my family, determined to not cheat anyone. I hardly know what I want. I decide to spend a few leisurely hours with Mom on Saturday afternoon, sitting on the patio of the nursing home, munching grapes and licking popsicles. "I'll bring her home another night," I console myself. "Sometimes it doesn't matter what she does, she's still miserable. She probably won't even remember the original plan." Her good days are becoming so infrequent that when those days arise, I don't want to disappoint her. But there is no way to know when a good day will present itself. Trying to live within the rollercoaster range of her moods can be emotionally devastating. There is no consistency, no way of predicting how she will be. Sadness courses through me. I'm starting to feel like that's all I have, inside. "Life's a bitch, and then you die."

On Saturday, I enter the nursing home carrying a bowl of seedless grapes and a cooler packed with Fudgsicles. Immediately, I'm struck by a hard-ball, the familiar smell of indignity–bodies that, through no choice of their own, are unable to control their human functions. I enter Mom's room. She smiles at me, pops up out of bed, slips into her shoes, and says, "Let's go!" She stands erect and nimbly guides her walker toward the door. "Oh shit!" I'm trembling. There it is. All that energy, all that spirit placed on hold for days on end, suddenly and completely let loose on a good day, when her brain resumes normal functioning. This is her Saturday, and I shrink from my task—both in awe of and threatened by this seething power. She is raring to go and I'm miserable, feeling horribly guilty about creating such an opportunity for disappointment.

I suggest, "Let's sit outside here on the patio awhile and enjoy the day. I've got grapes and treats!"

"It's a great day out," Mom says. "Not too hot." While we chat in the shade of the front terrace, Mom watches the comings and goings of birds and people. There is a nice breeze. It almost feels like our patio at home. Without discussion, we close our eyes and pretend we are elsewhere. We spend a couple of hours like this. I know dinner will be served on her floor, and that Tony and Amity will be waiting to go to the beach.

"Well, Mom, it's dinner-time here. Hungry? Guess I'll leave," I quickly suggest.

She says, "I thought I was coming to your house for dinner tonight." Damn it! She remembers.

"Well," I hesitate. "I thought we'd spend today together here. Turns out, um, we decided to sleep at the beach tonight so we can be there for a long day tomorrow. I'll be back in to visit on Monday."

Why did I wait so long to break the news? Did I really think she'd forgotten? Why didn't I just announce a postponement from the start? Am I ashamed to have fun if she can't? Do I think I can keep disappointment from her? She is already in a permanent state of disappointment. Why do I feel directly responsible for her happiness and guilty for her pain? Why do I deny things up until the last minute? I could have said, "Guess what, Mom? Tony, Amity, and I are going to the beach tonight! Won't that be nice for us? That way Amity and I can watch the sun come up on the beach and go bike riding early tomorrow morning. Remember when we used to do that? We'll make a bar-b-que next weekend. Okay?"

Instead I agonized through the afternoon, then finally told her before rushing away. I have become accustomed to the constant tremble of things going wrong. I can't give myself a break without suffering for it. I have begun to expect the worst and bring it on myself. Obviously, I am unable to confront disappointment head on—Mom's or my own. So, it comes in through the cellar, lasting longer. Like my Uncle Joe, Mom's eldest brother, who used to arrive at our basement door, drunk and singing, knowing full well my mother would give him five bucks to cover another drink and the carfare back to South Philadelphia. He never felt deserving enough to come in through the front door.

    I know that I'd like to change—perhaps get to the root of my own circumvention—instead I circumvent it. I watch Mom's spirit dissolve as my new plan registers. This is it, for her—the big day out is over. Her chin falls forward, her shoulders droop, and she disassociates, as I push her and her walker to the dining room. She accepts the role I have cast for her today. We kiss goodbye as the aides meet her with a wheel chair. I walk the long hall to the exit. I no longer notice the odor. It is the end of another long, hot day in the life of a nursing home—a prison in eternity for tired souls. I'm so torn. I can't please everyone. There is no way to know, no way to plan for her good days. On a bad day, she can crumble the best-laid plans. I can't take her to the beach, although I think about it. That would defeat the idea of a relaxing day for my family and me. But this hurts more.

    I drive to the beach feeling miserable and sick, while Tony plays with Amity in the backseat. I drive, absorbed in the deafening voices of my inner conflict. Could I have brought her? Why didn't we just leave on Sunday morning as planned? Why do I try to please everybody? I'm so tired of everything!

    I long to be in the ocean. I want the waves to rush over me, to untangle my hair and freshen my face. The ocean always renews me—like an old-fashioned doodle pad, when the top film is lifted, earlier designs dissolve. When we cross the bridge into Ocean City, it is the end of a long, hot day on the beach. Too bad we only have an hour or so left of daylight. If only we'd come earlier. I wonder if tomorrow will be as nice. Probably not. Already I feel a sense of loss, and we've just arrived. I make it clear that I want the ocean immediately. Amity comes with me. I bring along the book, *The Lovely Bones* by Alice Sebold, for beach reading, although I know I'll never get to it. Tony decides to find dinner. I figure he'll bring back a pizza for us to enjoy, oceanfront. Then I'll swim while he and Amity eat the pizza. I try to be patient as I play in the sand with Amity. As usual, she expects my mind to be wrapped around her play. But right now, it is anywhere but there. My eyes dart back and forth, watching for Tony's return from the boardwalk.

I need to swim! I can wait no longer. Amity is busy and self-sufficient. After about 45 minutes without Tony showing up, I decide to leave Amity alone digging in the sand while I get wet. There is no one else in sight. I decide to just keep an eye on her, while I swim. "Amity, honey, I'm going for a swim. Watch me in the ocean and I'll wave to you. You wave back, okay?"

"Uh, okay. But look at what I found!" The tiny white eggs she has uncovered beneath the wet sand fascinate her. She maintains her focus. I walk toward the shore.

I am angry with Tony for disappearing, at my mother for making me miserable, and at life for being so fucking hard! The sun moves further west. The salt-water embraces me, takes me into its shimmering arms, licks and coats me with healing salve. The further I venture, the freer I feel. Life's burdens and designs disappear. I submit, wanting more depth, more immersion, and more peace. "This is the life," I think. "I'm free." I think of Bruce Dern at the end of the movie, *Coming Home*, leaving his watch and clothes on the beach, he swims and disappears into the depths. I swim out further, indulging my thoughts. "I could just swim to China!" I giggle. As kids, we used to dig in the garden and think that if we kept digging we'd end up in China. Then I stop thinking, and feel the ocean wrapping its curls around me. The salt water washes over my lips and tongue, making me want to gargle and spit into the vast sea. My breath becomes shallow. I float above my body, it seems, and I like the feeling. I like the feeling of being alone–no thoughts, no responsibilities, and no life beyond this moment. The ocean filters my exhausted body through sand and salt. I'm fluid, all water and no mass, longing to merge with the porous, gyrating current surrounding me. Stay, stay with this moment I think, where there is no other reality—no shame, no guilt or pain, just air, water and depth; nothing but the moment and the stillness beyond the waves. See where it takes me. Where the blue ocean merges with the azure sky into something vaster than a simple lifetime, I gratefully surrender. Take me with you please, for I have no more to give.

And for an instant, my beautiful cousin Estelle appears. A gentle wave dips my body, submerges my face, kisses my lips with salt and pushes me back toward the land of the living, where a little girl waits for me. Instinctively, I extend my arm and swim a stroke, gulp some air over my right shoulder, and notice Amity—a silhouette, still playing in the sand with the sun behind her. Her shadow reaches toward me. My heart swells with a sense of urgency more powerful than the need to be free. I need to be her mother. I swim toward her, feeling suddenly caffeinated. My altered senses release the dam of memory. I smell the Noxzema, taste salt, chew sand, and search for loud-colored Florida towels featuring buxom gals in scant bikinis—towels smelling like Tide, spread and flattened by the fat, familiar bodies of my aunts and cousins of ample bosom in ruffled, one-piece, skirted bathing suits, dipping pretzels into mustard.

My mother's sisters beckon from the beach, offering themselves to me, willing to help me—to take my place with this child, if that is truly what I want. Better yet, they are happy to take my suffering. "Let me take that from you, Sweetheart. You need to be happy. I don't. Here, I'll take your pain."

"No, no let me take it!" My aunts are jockeying to absorb my pain, just like they would fight to pay the nickel for the Tacony Palmyra Bridge on the way to the beach.

"Here, here, I got the nickel!"

"No, put it away! I got it!"

"Put away your pain, Sweetheart. I got it!" Their voices dissolve, but the comfortable feeling of their presence remains. I must give Amity the comfort that I have received in this lifetime. I must transmit the blessings of a loving family. I am not my mother, or her supportive sisters and nieces, but I can give her my gifts. She will have the confidence that comes from knowing she is loved. I will not choose to take that away from her. I swim back to the shore to embrace Amity's body–warm and delicious, still absorbed in the mysteries of the life beneath the sand. I shake off the residue of what I might have done, and settle back onto solid ground. I look up through my tears to see Tony, approaching with a pizza.

"Where were you? I wanted to swim. You knew that!" I'm still angry with him for the delay.

"I took my time. I didn't think you needed me," Tony submits, surprised by my ire. I know I need him. I need the sustenance and pleasure of his presence, as much as I need Amity and the pizza. For the rest of the weekend, I choose to enjoy my family and let them know it. I drive home determined not to cheat anyone, not even myself.

Intercession

Fall, 2003

Mom needs more care, and the money is dwindling. She can't stay where she is when her money runs out. It is a private facility, chosen for its convenience to my house. I need to find a place that has what are called "sniff beds." Apparently, this is how professionals in health care refer to beds reserved for folks who are out of money and receive Medicaid benefits to pay for nursing care. I can't imagine that most people have ten thousand dollars a month lying around to pay for their care. What's more, with Medicaid benefits you must be "lucky" enough to find a sniff bed in a nice place. Lucky people don't spend their last days on Medicaid in a nursing home. But lowering expectations of what is desirable and lucky seems to be what you do in this situation.

The county home is the option of last resort. If you have nowhere else to go, they must take you. I can only imagine the forgotten people stockpiled there. It's far away from my house and everyone else Mom knows, although no one but me, and sometimes my brothers, visits her anymore. She'll just take up space in a warehouse for lost souls. How can I let this happen? How could anyone let this happen? I've always thought of Mom's deceased sisters as her guardian angels. Gone, but still connected on another plane. Now, I'm beginning to think that nothing is out there. No one watches over us. If they did, they would never let this happen. They would never leave her here, so depressed and unhappy, to suffer the indignity and madness of a shriveling mind. They would fight over her dying mind, take it away from her and give her peace. Certainly, if there is any type of benevolent force in the universe, any kind of eternal memory watching all this play out on Earth, how could they not stop this? Why would they not intercede?

Mom grew up the ninth of ten children. With a family of this size, coming of age during the Great Depression, there was always a sense of community and a built-in support system. Beginning at age 14, everyone worked to keep the family solvent and they all had jobs within the household. Aunt Jean did the family's laundry with a washboard and basin. Aunt Lena had been the most successful breadwinner, always securing the best jobs. Aunt Bess took care of the younger kids. This is how they grew. Each married, established a home, settled close to each other, and continued the support by caring for each other's families. Our neighbors became part of the extended family. Mom attracted people because she had the confidence and generous spirit that came from being raised in a household of givers. Her community has disintegrated piece by piece over time. As one of the last surviving members of her generation, Mom is left with remnants, frayed threads from a tightly woven life. Her heavily wrinkled face reflects all that she has known and lost.

I grew up watching home movies of our family—my mother and father their parents, brothers and sisters, younger versions of this older generation, cavorting for the camera. Uncle Harry, Aunt Bessie, Aunt Lena—their forty-year old bodies entangled in a pyramid on the living room floor, collapse on top of each other in hysterics. Bessie chugs from an endless, empty bottle of booze. Cousin Howard, Robyn's father in a double-fisted frenzy, eats his way across the bounteous dining room table. These films of our elders "hamming it up" created a silly, sweet, and referential family mythology. The films became our memories as family members died. Even as the films began disintegrating, Sheldon, my eldest brother who changed his name to Steve upon adulthood, would splice together what was left, and the act of splicing, along with the glitches created, became part of our story. I remember a scene of my parents in a long embrace and passionate kiss that Sheldon would project and freeze on the frame where their lips met. The audience of kid cousins and neighbors pointed and shrieked, held their noses and said "Eeeewwwww!" while some of the older boys yelled to my on-screen father "Go Abie Go!" The freeze frame, the screaming, the subsequent splitting of the film followed by the repetitive whip, whip, whipping, of the broken piece circling the reel, cued Sheldon to throw on the lights and bring out the splicing kit, and the rest of us to grab a Tastykake from the kitchen. The living room filled with the noxious fumes of the bonding solvent that stung your nostrils like a mix of airplane glue and plastic bubbles from a tube, while my brother aligned the two end pieces of film on a tray, fixed them together with an additional piece of celluloid and painted on the stinking glue. Once the splice dried, we returned to the show. Eventually the kiss disintegrated under the stress of so many splices, but the embrace remained bracketing the gap.

Now, as my mother's memory and life disintegrates and I scurry to splice together the remains, my heart is feeling the lack of endurable substance. I realize that nothing lasts forever, and I'm beginning to think that there is nothing beyond what we see or understand. Life happens and then you die, with precious little to splice together at the end. Perhaps each of us is all alone and terrified, so we imagine connections that don't really exist. It keeps us happy, although I'm not so happy anymore. The same things that once defined Mom now haunt her. The other night, "Why Did I Choose You", Barbra Streisand from 1965—a favorite song, particularly poignant because Mom dedicated it to Dad at his funeral in 1992—came on the radio just as she landed her butt on the cold ground after missing the wheelchair.

"Shut that the hell off!" she demanded, cursing from a gravelly patch beside the car for the duration of the song. I scrambled for help to lift her. I soon learned that the caregivers who work inside nursing homes are not allowed to help people negotiate the parking lot. That's up to the family.

I remember how Mom would stop whatever she was doing back in the 1960s, whenever she heard Anthony Newley belting out his Grammy-winning song, "What Kind of Fool Am I?" He wrote and introduced this song in the musical, *Stop the World: I Want to Get Off*. The other day, the movie version played on the TV in the day room. It was easy to leave after visiting Mom knowing that soon she'd be swept up in that song. But just after I left, I received a call.

"Tracy, your mom just fell forward from her wheel chair, and hit the floor flat on her face. She's bruised, but okay. We will be seating her in a reclining wheel chair from now on. Don't worry, she's fine." Mom's favorite Broadway musicals now provide the soundtrack to her nightmare. In fact, "Stop the world: I want to get off!" is exactly what she has been demanding of us for the past year! Considering her lifelong resonance with the theater, I can't help but wonder whether her fall was more of a jump.

A psychologist is making the rounds at the nursing home. He is her age, has the same background, and actually grew up in the same South Philly neighborhood. I'm excited. I think, "Here's someone who might reach her, someone to whom she might confide." I make an appointment. I'm looking forward to it. These days, I'm grappling for a savior.

"Sylvia, how are you feeling? Vos makhstu?" he asks. He speaks in Yiddish, the language of their parents, attempting to bond.

"Go to hell, you fucking bastard! Who do you think you are, anyway?" Mom responds.

I fall back in my chair, wowed by Mom's unexpected facility with the language of my youth. Not hers. When I was growing up, Mom forbade us to curse in the house. "In our family, we don't curse," she'd say. She insisted we find another word that was more descriptive and less foul. My response as a rebellious teenager was to substitute "fucking" for every adjective I knew.

"She thinks I'm an old flame from the past. Women often do," the doctor says. He seems flattered. I don't know what she thinks. How would he? I think he doesn't know her at all. And I'm not sure who's more senile. I can't hold back my tears of deep disappointment in both of them.

"Don't cry," he says. "This happens with dementia. I knew a demented rabbi who cursed like a sailor. People say crazy things— things they never would have uttered when they were well."

I want to say, "So what's your excuse?" but he locks up his briefcase, signaling the end of our session. I watch him, from our usual spot on the terrace, teetering back to his car after making his rounds. He drives an old Lincoln Continental–big and boxy the way Mom liked her cars. I can tell from his car that they are cut from the same cloth; they grew up with the same values and influences, and once had the same dreams. I wonder what force controls fortune, and why one 84-year-old walks away and drives home in style, enjoying the fruits of his life's labors, while another sits with head in hands on a nursing home terrace, never to go home again.

I encourage my eldest brother, Steve (formerly Sheldon,) who now lives in California, to come and visit Mom, before she declines any further. He has not been home since her illness began, although he has received my reports and has expressed his concern. At each change of her status or new decision concerning her health and wellbeing, I have notified Steve along with my two other brothers. Up until now his response has been, "I'm not there. You are. I support your decision." Now, he will come for two weeks and see for himself. He'll stay with my family and me, and perhaps visit with her every day in her nearby room at the nursing home. I'm a bit concerned as to whether I'll end up caring for him as well. What I don't need now, is a needy houseguest. He has suffered from colitis, mental depression and anger issues for many years. Mom has always been his rock.

Steve was the first-born of the four siblings in my family. He grew to middle age with strong, vital parents who provided a safety net for him—extending money, time, and a mature perspective to floundering life decisions and bouts of bad luck. Even now, I don't think Steve truly realizes how much the tables have turned on us. The second eldest, Lanse, was always self-directed with a strong interest in science and building racecars. He didn't present too many problems as a kid, and for now he's content with not getting too involved. My younger brother, Myles, and I had middle-aged parents when we were young, and experienced more of their vulnerability, not that this stopped us from rebelling against them or making bad decisions. But I think that the acceptance of this change in Mom has been more gradual for the younger siblings, and I'm feeling the need to protect Steve from the contrast that he is about to experience.

  I recognize Steve up ahead, seated on a curbside bench as I pull into the USAir quick-pick-up lane at Philadelphia International Airport. His prized blonde hair has thinned and darkened to scattered brown patches. He looks crumpled and exhausted but his head rotates as his expectant eyes fix on each approaching car and follow it away in disappointment. I pull up and he looks worried, extending his neck and straining his brow to inspect my car, but when his eyes set on mine he smiles. Like Myles, Steve inherited our father's blue eyes and they comfort me in this moment. His jacket, newspapers and carry-on bag are splayed across the bench that he has appropriated. Three suitcases surround him. Together, we load the car with his possessions. I attribute his jerking movements and exaggerated facial expressions to side effects from the prescribed narcotics he has been dependent on for several years.

  "How are you," I ask as he settles into the passenger's seat beside me.

  "Well, my stomach problems continue and I'm in the bathroom for at least two hours every morning."

  "Umm, the guest room has a private bath, so you'll be okay."

  "Listen Trace, I'm really determined to set my problems aside, while I'm here to help you with Mom. In fact, I've brought two suitcases full of videos to watch with her. Do you think she'll like that?"

  "I think with you, she'll like that."

This all sounds promising and I'm excited for Mom to have the undivided attention of her eldest child. It is late afternoon by the time I've retrieved my brother from the airport and whisk him over to the dementia unit. The crisp, clean fall air that our entrance admits turns sour and oppressive as we cross the lobby to Mom's hallway. Meanwhile, it's "Happy Hour" for all residents willing and able to participate. A tuxedoed piano player warbles show tunes and old standards from the 1940s, while the clinking of trembling hands gripping icy cold glasses of old familiar beverages shatters the silence between the beats. A nasal cocktail of stale urine and steely disinfectant dulls our brains and prepares us for the lethargy beyond the lobby. I spy Mom slumped in her wheelchair, disassociated, head in her lap, as we approach the front of the nurses' station. I'm wondering if Steve recognizes her. I'm feeling ashamed for her, and disappointed for him.

"Mom! Look who's here!" I greet my mother as if we're arriving at her house for Sunday brunch. Her heavy head rises in slight increments as if lifted by a pulley. It looks like all her surviving muscle tone has converged to her neck to assist the task. Mom looks up, recognizes her first born immediately, smiles, cries and just about hops out of her chair to embrace him.

"How about it, Trace. Let's get outa here," she insists.

We experience another blessing and for the next couple of weeks, I get an emotional break knowing that Steve is keeping her busy, showing her movies, and engaging her in familiar conversation. In the evenings, he shuttles her to my house, while I prepare family dinners of cheese blintzes with strawberries and sour crème. This works for Amity and Tony, so long as the good mood lasts. Toward the end of his stay, Steve tells me that it's getting harder and harder to transfer Mom from her wheelchair to the car and back out again. Would I mind driving her back to her room in the evening after dinner? So, I pick up the slack for him, which disrupts my bedtime ritual with Amity.

Steve returns home to California after two helpful and otherwise uneventful weeks. After which, Mom, for the most part, returns to her former state. I'm not surprised. It is her pattern to gather all her resources and rise to an occasion. She simply cannot hold on to the feeling without constant one-on-one attention, the kind that is also impossible to sustain.

I remember a day back at The Protestant Home when David, a family friend and professional musician visited, carting an electric piano and a box of chocolates. He performed a private concert of popular music and big band standards in Mom's room. She smiled, clapped and rose in her seat, dancing, swaying and singing along to "Someday, when you're awfully low, when the world is cold..." The hits never stopped and neither did Mom for an hour and a half. At the end Mom yelled "Bravo, bravo!" She thanked David and his attentive wife, Debbie, with huge hugs and kisses.

When they left, she collapsed in her chair, turned to me, and in a tone that sounded almost accusatory said, "So, who's coming tomorrow?"

In retrospect, I realize that her question was just another commentary on my naiveté. Mom knew early on the trajectory of her illness. She knew that I would keep applying Band-Aids to a wound that would never heal. And that perhaps, I would never be able to stare plainly at the wound, without applying salve. But I have moved a little closer to acknowledging her fate. I have put Mom's name on the list of several nursing homes that have sniff beds. I am concerned that as she continues to fail, her funds from the sale of the house will run out, and then where will she be? Hopefully not back at my house, or the county home. My mind is once again off and running with possibilities. And the good ones continue to fall.

I lie awake in bed at night, in a state between sleeping and waking. My mantra these days is: Life sucks, then you die. I keep coming back to that. I have finally come to the end of my inherited and inherent optimism. I have nothing else to give. I don't dream anymore. I think. I still listen for my mother or my daughter's voice needing assistance in the middle of the night. I plan, review, and ruminate. I hear neighborhood cats fighting until— my deep sigh admits the lighter air of dawn. My body welcomes the change. My nostrils flare and lungs expand. My mind relaxes and travels.

Amity and I are sitting by a stream. Amity fades, and Aunt Jean is sitting next to me, wearing her hand-crocheted black-and-white sweater. She reads. The air is saturated with—Aunt Jean-ness—a splash of Jean Nate, the scent of nail polish. I am filled with a presence, her spirit–what it felt like to be with her. Yet I know I am still in my bed.

"Aunt Jean!! Jeanie!!!" I want to shout, smiling from ear-to-ear, like I am greeting her at her house for dinner. But she is gone. In that moment—that flash of recognition—she touches pursed lips to my forehead. I absorb this comfort. It courses through me. It was a prayer book she was reading, I think. She was reading the "Kaddish," the Jewish Prayer for the Dead. She came to tell me that there will be death, and healing. I feel lighter. It's not all on me. This is the intercession that I have been waiting for. I feel embraced, once again. I am a part of something greater than myself. I'll be able to sleep now, and soon rejoin the land of the living.

I call Mom's room after rising. A caregiver answers. "I'm having a hard time getting your mother up and dressed. She won't stop crying," she tells me.

"See if she'll talk to me," I suggest.

Mom gets on the phone. "Mom, how about it?" I tell her. "I'll take you out for Chinese food tonight! I'll come at six."

Mom cries out, half-asleep, angry and scared, "I'm dying. I know it. I'm dying today. Oh, Trace, I'm going to die!"

I wonder, while Aunt Jean was in the neighborhood, could she have planted the same heavenly kiss on Mom? The only difference is that for Mom, waking up is the nightmare.

This heavenly visitation has allowed us to turn a corner. Something great has happened. I feel lucky. Or perhaps it is simply that my definition of "luck" has changed. Mom has been accepted into Martins Run—a nearby, reputable, well-run retirement community with sniff beds. She can remain in this nursing home for however long she lives. She will move there in December. I tell Mom about the move, trying to make it sound like it is worth the effort.

"Martins Run is a Jewish place, Mom. And since you'll be there in December, you won't have to put up with all the Christmas…"

"Mishegas!" she pipes in, meaning craziness. I guess she doesn't mind moving.

Bravo

December, 2003

Mom doesn't die. She moves to Martins Run Retirement Community. The change of environment seems to invigorate her. She expresses the desire to exercise, and attends a music program. "The Yiddish songs remind me of Grandpop," she says. On New Year's Day, I decide to bring her to my house for our annual brunch. In between party preparations, I drive to Martins Run to fetch Mom. The aides lift her out of bed with what looks like an overhead crane with hooks. Mom looks as oriented as a slab of meat while she is hoisted out of bed and maneuvered into a wheelchair. But I bring Tony's "Cousin Cissy, the artist," with me, whom Mom has always admired for her talent and independence. As soon as Mom recognizes her, she begins chatting with her guest. She becomes increasingly animated during the ride to my house—happy to be out and celebrating the New Year, 2004. I settle her into a cozy and prominent chair in the living room. She smiles and greets our guests as they arrive. She eats hot dogs with mustard, onions, pepper hash and sauerkraut—a family comfort food. She holds court with family and friends—calling everyone "Sweetheart!" for the rest of the day.

On the following three days, I have weddings to photograph so I depend on the nursing home care. On the fourth day, I visit and can tell instantly that she's had another stroke. Her face is crooked and her bottom dentures jut out. The jutting false teeth underscore her misery, anger, and the under-bite that was always an embarrassment. Now my mother looks the part of monster in a nightmare from which she cannot separate. I call the doctor, who confirms my suspicions of stroke.

"How would you treat this?" I ask.

"We could admit her to the hospital and..." He drones on about procedures to sustain her, which I know will only prolong her discomfort and despair.

"No extreme measures. It's not her wish," I say.

Two weeks after that, Aunt Lena, now 96, still holding her own in Florida and following Mom's illness with interest and concern, catches pneumonia. Rapidly, her lungs fill with fluid. Her doctor calls to ask me if we should go to extremes to possibly revive her. (I have also become her power of attorney since Mom got sick.) Lena may end up hooked to a machine. I know she would not want that.

"No, it's not her wish. No extreme measures," I say. I have now given the instruction to "pull the plug" on the last two Kravitz siblings—the "grown-ups" of our family. One month after the intercession, Aunt Lena is dead.

I visit Mom just after receiving the news. I feel it's my responsibility to tell her right away. Despite Mom's physical and mental losses, she has not lost the ability to love or mourn her family. She expresses her love whenever she has a clear moment. Mom is Aunt Lena's closest surviving relation. From their immediate family of 13, Mom alone, is left to do the mourning. I want to mourn Aunt Lena with Mom. I'm still seeking the comfort that she once provided. I had imagined that Mom would die before Lena considering the circumstances, and that I'd be traveling to Florida to give Aunt Lena the news. We would comfort each other. I wonder why Aunt Lena, who was 96 and still enjoying her life in relatively good health, had to go first. Was this some cosmic sacrifice Aunt Lena made, to give her younger sister permission to die? Did Jean visit Lena as well?

I'm scared to tell Mom about Lena. Will she freak out? Can she get any more depressed? Will she bite me? I don't know what to expect. I inform the staff of Lena's death. An aide decides to sit with me in Mom's room, while I break the news. Perhaps she'll be helpful if Mom becomes combative.

I set up a little picnic of treats on a table between Mom and me. We munch on grapes and pretzels. I chat for too long about the weather, my daughter, and the nursing home food. I'm trying to find a comfortable place from which to break the news. As usual, I'm avoiding the unpleasant inevitable. Finally, I say, "Mom, remember I told you Aunt Lena was in the hospital with pneumonia? How Sondra (our Bess's daughter) flew in from California to be with her?"

"I'm glad Sondra's with her," she says.

"Well, as soon as Sondra arrived, Lena noticed she was there, then passed away. Aunt Lena died, Mom!" I say, looking directly in her eyes.

Her placid, hazel eyes grow large, wild and unreachable. She looks outraged and her eyes seem to say, "How dare you tell me this? How dare she go and not me!!" She looks so angry I think she might hit me. But she blinks and her face changes. She breaks into tears and we embrace and cry as we might have years before. Now I'm sorry that the aide is with us. It's an unnecessary intrusion. I feel like saying to this staff person, "Aunt Lena died! How can you just sit there not reacting, if you're gonna sit here with us, react with us!" It's just that this is such an honest moment, allowing us to penetrate the lacquered fortress of Mom's dementia.

I hold a memorial service for Lena at Martins Run, so Mom can attend. I rent the party room, have it catered, and invite cousins and friends, young and old to celebrate Lena's life. I set up a TV/VCR and show footage of Lena fielding autobiographical questions that I had recorded ten years previous. The young cousins are drawn to this, getting to know Aunt Lena electronically, as she speaks about going to dances as a young woman in the 1920s. Lena delights in listing the names of men she dated—like Herman Berman, which cracks us all up. She sighs as she mentions settling down with Harry, then perks up as she recalls their successful business. I'm reminded that once again we're keeping the elders alive through home movies.

Meanwhile, once all the guests have arrived, I roll Mom in, in a chair that looks like a Barcalounger on wheels. Since she can't sit erect without the possibility of disassociating and falling forward flat on her face, the new chair angles her backward in permanent recline. The adults are drawn to her, though I can see many terrified faces in the crowd, having not seen Mom since her condition worsened. They approach her tentatively. Mom smiles in recognition of the parade of familiar faces passing in front of her and greets nieces, nephews and friends by name. But if anyone comes too close or speaks too long or loud, she loses patience and screams, "Enough! Get out of here!" and the crowd shifts backwards.

So, we have Lena chatting amicably on one side of the room, dead and gone but well preserved on videotape; and Mom on the other side, wishing as much for herself. But when the crowd recedes and three of her four children sit beside her, Mom starts eating cookies, laughing, flirting with her sons, and visibly enjoying this party. Steve is in from California. We wonder where Lanse is, since he lives nearby. "Guess he had to work," I say. This excuse, which has always been status quo in our family (Dad always "had to work," missing countless family events,) doesn't carry its usual weight. We feel the importance of this moment, and miss Lanse's presence. Myles sits beside Mom the whole time holding her hand. Steve, Myles, and I stay later than the rest of the guests, enjoying what may well be, Mom's last party.

I return to Martins Run the next day. Mom is miserable and incommunicado. In the days that follow, she stops eating for good. I can't watch, as she fights the aides, seals her lips or spits back her food. Again, I try to stop the inevitable. Every day, I bring in irresistible black-and-white milk shakes—a blender mix of Breyers vanilla ice cream, whole milk and Hershey's syrup with a flexible straw. She can't resist. It's the only thing that crosses her lips. My milkshakes sustain her throughout the miserable month of February and into March. Then her heart rate soars and her doctor recommends that she not leave her bed for fear that the additional stress will cause a heart attack. I wonder would that be so bad? Although on most days, getting up isn't something she wants to do anyway.

However, on a warm Thursday in early March, when I enter her room, "Tracela!" she greets me. "Look at this little boy. He's so adorable!" She points toward the TV. She's watching *Ellen* and clearly interested. There is a caregiver named Molly in the room watching over Mom's roommate. Molly sits erect against the wall to my left with her hands folded as if in prayer over the large pocketbook in her lap. I greet her and the still body in the bed that is her charge. Molly keeps motioning with her chin towards Mom's bed across the room and smiling back at me. She keeps shaking her head. At first I think she's got a surprise gift for me inside that purse, the way she's protecting it, but then I realize the gift is Mom. I hear Molly say under her breath, "Oh merciful God." Mom is sitting up in bed, alert and laughing. She seems to be aware of everything around her, and it is all a source of joy.

"It's beautiful out! Let's go for a walk. How 'bout it, Trace? It's getting to be spring!" Mom says. She bends her knees, shifts her body towards me, dangles her legs over the side of the bed frame and looks around for her shoes. She's practically singing her words. "Sooooo, when do I go home?" she asks. Her voice is nonchalant but mindful, bright, breezy and clear as the day. It's as if the nightmare of the last few years has never happened; as if she is recuperating from some minor event, and as if home—her beloved Eastwood Street home—awaits her recovery.

"When your heart rate goes down, you'll go home," I say trying to sound as unaffected by present circumstances as she is. I know what to do. I get a wheelchair and lift her into it. She doesn't weigh much. We wheel through the garden, watching birds in flight. The air is perfumed by the earliest of flowers. Mom follows butterflies with her eyes, smiles as the wind rustles her hair, and lifts her cheek to the breeze. After being cooped up in an airless institution and a dried-up, dysfunctional body, suddenly Mom's circuits are firing and her senses are immersed in the moment.

It's hard to leave her, but I've promised Amity and the boys next door that I'd pick them up early from after-care and we'd bake pastries for Purim. They love rolling out the dough—a refrigerated mixture of flour, cream cheese and butter—cutting it into small circles, plopping the filling in the center, folding each to resemble a three-cornered hat, and squeezing the corners till they stick.

"I'm going home to bake hamantashen with the kids now, Mom. Remember the prune with nuts we'd eat hot from the oven?" Hamantashen was a prized recipe of hers.

"Yum! Save some for me!" Mom gives a smile of guilty pleasure, wishing me luck with the baking. "Yours are always so much neater than mine," she adds, keeping me a little longer.

I counter, "That's 'cause the cherry filling is more manageable than the prune, and you like eating the prune while you're making them." This is a repetition of an on-going, 35-year conversation about hamantashen.

By the following Monday, she is struggling to breathe. I recognize the death rattle; a gurgling in her throat that says her lungs are full of fluid, and death is imminent. I keep calling in the floor nurse and asking what I can do to help her to breathe. The nurse checks her vitals and makes sure she is as comfortable as possible.

"She's getting ready to go," she says softly, almost afraid to break the news to me. I can't really process what she is saying anyway. "She's getting ready to go..." Mom has been "ready to go" for a long time and she goes nowhere. Not that I want her to. I still want her to recover! I know that death is imminent, but I'm used to dealing with the next crisis, which is what this feels like. I don't know what the final stage will feel like and I don't want to know. I only know that something new is happening with Mom—something that feels, finally very normal, and I feel an urgency to say something about it to her. I lean in close, sensing a presence beside me, sharing a sudden feeling of triumph over our dementia.

"Mom," I whisper. "Whatever this was—this curse on the last few years—for whatever reason it happened, you got through it. It's over now. You stuck it out to the end. Bravo, Mom. Bravo!"

I'm remembering my mother's habit at the curtain of a theater performance she'd enjoyed, of applauding non-stop and emoting, "Bravo!" She would stand and applaud in appreciation until the orchestra played their last note and then blow kisses at them, always the last one to leave the theater. I wonder if she gets my "Bravo!" reference.

Mom smiles, winks at me, and silently claps her hands together. She seems relieved. I am letting her go.

"Bye Mom, I'm going home to make dinner. Cousin Cissy is coming over! See you tomorrow," I say.

She can't talk, but she looks at me with that familiar mix of concern and disbelief. She knows I won't see her tomorrow. How could I not know? How could I be so naïve? I just assume that the dying will go on and on, like every other stage in this merciless illness. I selfishly want it to. I am attached even to this. But her eyes let go of their concern for me, as she struggles to breathe. I miss my cue. I go home to make dinner for my family. And at one o'clock the next morning, I receive the call that Mom has followed our Lena in death.

I return to her room at Martins Run to sit with her body until the collector from Goldstein's Funeral Home arrives. "Hi Mom." I greet her and kiss her cold forehead. Her familiar body lies frozen in death in that same bed, with the same unmoved roommate, lightly breathing in the other. Mom's eyes are rolled back into her head. Her mouth has dropped wide open, as if determined for that one last breath. "I'm going to sit here and meditate now, and keep you company until Goldstein's arrives." I settle into a chair by her bed and cross my legs in front of me. I wish I had been positioned here, holding her hand when she died, and I think I might be trying to make up for it now. I imagine she was wondering why I wasn't. But as usual, my optimism and naïveté prevailed. And Mom wouldn't have directly asked me to be there with her

Although, she might have said, "How 'bout it, Trace?"

Di Gantse Velt Iz Sheyn — The Whole World is Beautiful

March 9, 2004

Seven years after driving Mom to the cemetery on a warm September morning lifetimes ago, I stand by a mound where her monument will be. It's a windy day in March. She is the last of her generation to die. There are no aunts or uncles left, just cousins. Today I have been driven here along with Tony and Amity, in a limousine that Mom included in her pre-paid funeral package. Cousin Miriam (Aunt Jean's granddaughter) and her son Steven rode along with us. All three of my brothers surround me, their spouses and children, and Bessie's son Denny and his family. Ben and Eva's daughter Sandee, and son Stephen are here. They are the siblings of Mom's beloved niece, Estelle. Other nieces and nephews, the children of Mom and Dad's other siblings are also here. We are the grown-ups now, adult cousins encircling her coffin of solid pine. We each toss some dirt on top, some with a shovel and others preferring to soil their hands. Then we wipe our hands clean because we are no longer children, and we know that we could dig in the dirt all day and never reach China, or have our mother back.

A bench has been erected nearby which says "Kauffman." I remember Mom mentioning it when we stopped at that diner for lunch seven years ago, after visiting her parents' gravestones—the day she stood by their monuments, channeled them for me, and spoke to them of her beautiful world. I'm silently amused by how proud she was of her thoughtful burial plan. "...So you'll always have a place to sit and cry," she said. Perhaps I will someday, but today I shed no tears. I am relieved for my mother and for myself. The funeral is the normal part. This is the day for which I've been waiting. Her mind and her body are dead at the same time. I will never understand the indignity of the last few years– why we had to witness such unbearable loss. Perhaps the dignity lies in having navigated it together.

I notice that Amity is without her jacket. She forgot it in her excitement to ride in the limousine. The critical voice in my head is Aunt Bessie's: "Who brings a child to the cemetery without a coat?" Feeling guilty and exposed as a neglectful mother, I take off my coat and wrap it around my daughter. My cousin notices me without my coat. She takes off her coat and wraps it around me. Her son notices his mother, coatless, and wraps her in his. We coat each other. We've been handed down a fabric that sustains us. I hear my mother's chirpy voice repeat the words I watched her speak to her dead mother in a cemetery seven years ago, "Di gantse velt iz sheyn." This time I need no translation.

One More Day

It is Wednesday, my day to write. I begin by journaling in my car, parked in the lot of a busy shopping center. I'm trying to freely associate the surrounding sounds and smells of the parking lot with whatever impressions come up for me. Nothing comes. Determined to find meaning from memories, I struggle and mine for depth in my imperceptible scrawl. I'm yearning for the seamless flow from impression to insight to expression. What I really need is a bathroom break. I leave the car and walk to the bagel shop. Perhaps a cup of coffee will get me started, I think upon entering.

"Sweetheart!" she calls out to me from in front of the candy counter. "Let's indulge!" Zapped from my silent musings, my body trembles and my eyes confirm what my heart never doubted.

"Ma?" It comes out more like a quack than a human sound. "Ma, you're dead! How are you here?" No one else seems to hear me. My sounds lack breath.

"C'mon Trace. Let's indulge. How 'bout those chocolate pretzels with the nonpareils? They really have nice stuff here." She winks at me, licking her lips. She appears childlike and energetic, hell-bent on having fun. This was my mother, before depression, dementia and death came between us. What do you say when your dead mother shows up demanding chocolate?

"Mom, maybe we ought to have lunch first," I suggest. "Chinese food?" I ask, raising my eyebrows in co-conspiracy. She likes that.

"Trace, you always know the right way to do things." I allow her compliment to sink in. My mother and her older sisters used to praise me for simple things. I always brushed it off, wondering what the big deal was. Now, that all of them have died, there is nowhere I can go for such easy As in life.

I miss them. Mom and I leave Delancey Street Bagels. We hold hands and skip across the parking lot toward The China House. She opens the door for me, then plops herself into a booth.

"I'll have won ton soup, shrimp in lobster sauce and an egg roll please," she announces to me, and the waiter, not wasting any time.

"I'll have the same." I follow her lead, suspending all logic, reason and doubt to savor the moment.

"Trace, you never order that!" She seems flattered. "But it's a shame, we could've shared one dish."

"Do you want me to call the waiter back?" I ask.

"Oh no, no." She waives the thought away. "So, what's new, Sweetheart?" What's new? Where should I start? What can I say to her? A million things and nothing that seems as important as the fact that she sits across from me in a booth at a Chinese restaurant.

"Maybe I should ask you 'What's new?' Mom?" With a fried noodle, she scoops up the remains on her plate, and then works on mine.

"Aren't you going to finish your shrimp, Trace?" She feigns concern as she pops another one of my shrimps in her mouth. Her clothes are familiar; bright, colorful and unstained as from before her illness. She wears orange lipstick and a necklace of plastic daisies. Matching flowers cover her earlobes, clipping on in the back. She reeks of Secret of Venus, the perfume she favored when I was a child. I bask in her fragrance, reminiscent of dinners out and nights on the town. Between that, the chirping of her voice and the sense of adventure that envelops us, I'm willing to believe that time, space and mortal affliction have been transcended. I wonder what I should tell her about our family, friends, her grandchildren and her beloved home. How much does she already know?

"Do you have today's paper, and dessert?" she asks the waiter. I'm surprised that current events are important to her. "See what's at the theater, Trace. We could probably just make a two o'clock matinee. Seen any good shows lately?" I confess that I've been too busy to keep up her legacy of loyal theater patronage.

"Besides work and family, I have my writing now, Mom."

"Good for you! I'm proud of you. Writing is in our family. But you need inspiration. I always feel great when I'm watching a show. Let's grab that chocolate and head downtown."

We arrive at the Academy of Music in time for the matinee. The show is *Wicked*. I've seen it before but I always longed to share it with Mom. Since her death, whenever I sit in the audience of a theater, it seems like she is embracing me at the high points. When I saw *Peter Pan* with Cathy Rigby, my eyes brimmed with her happy tears. When I yelled, "Beautiful, beautiful! Bravo!" to the orchestra, I knew she inhabited me. I'm wondering now if this day isn't all in my head. Perhaps I'm alone at the theater feeling her presence as before, and I'm imagining the rest of this crazy scenario? Mom breaks off a piece of the chocolate pretzel and places it into my mouth. She finishes the rest and drops the bag as the curtain rises. There is no denying Mom. She is here, defying gravity and every other natural law.

At intermission, I speed to the bathroom and return with M&Ms. "Wow! They make them with almonds, now." Mom is ecstatic. We hold hands through the denouement, and clap for the orchestra until their final note. "Beautiful, beautiful, Bravo!" she cups her hands and yells into the orchestra pit.

We exit the empty theater singing, "Defying Gravity" and float toward the parking lot.

"Should I drive you home now, Mom?" I'm feeling brave and giddy from the day. If she can materialize healthy and strong, why can't her beloved house? She left it one day, in a demented moment, never to return from what I called, assisted dying. Certainly, today feels more real and right, than her last sick years ever did.

"I'm home Sweetheart, and it's good. But it's not life. There is nothing like life. Nothing. It's too short. It happens in a day like today. Short and sweet. Enjoy it. Fill it with chocolate, Chinese food and days on the town. How 'bout it? You didn't need me to tell you this, but as usual I couldn't resist the temptation. Thanks, Trace, for giving me one more day."

Appendix

Bubbe Ida at the hot dog cart on South 4th Street in South Philadelphia

Friday night at Bubbe's 1967
Row 1, l to r: Minnie, Sondra.
Row 2, l to r: Lily, Bessie, Lena, Sylvia

Sylvia and Tracy 1961

Disney World, February 2000

Family Gathering October 2003

Acknowledgments

My mother spoke to me in full sentences from day one, and read to me every night. My father loved the English language, although it was not his first, and read English poetry to us on his limited days off. Around the house, we spoke in grammatically correct sentences with an expected facility in English. Books were abundant, as were photographs, conversation, and good food. I am so grateful for these early influences.

Thank you to Ellen Szabo and my first writing group, where I hit the ground running. The Iowa Summer Writing Workshop was formative, and kudos to Nancy Barry for the initial and continued encouragement. I found an audience at Womensmemoirs.com, with help from Matilda Butler and Kendra Bonnett, making all the difference. Naomi Rose's editing skills brought this story to the next level. And there's nothing like having a copy editor in the family for an informed read. I'm grateful to Cousin Diana Rose. Cousin Shelley Fine's support as my Yiddish consultant was so appreciated and such fun. At Rosemont College with Richard Bank, I honed a series of vignettes into a manuscript. Richard's support and enthusiastic foreword to this book has brought it to the point of publication. He has earned his pepper hash. Cindy Glass Weinraub, a devoted reader and friend, inspires my craft because she "gets" me. I am also grateful for the feedback and endorsement from Robin Schneller-Frankwich, who has taken the elder care journey both professionally and personally. B. E. (Betti) Kahn's honest, poetic expression inspires me for the long haul. This collective encouragement, enthusiasm and feedback has launched a lifetime pursuit.

I feel much gratitude toward Dr. Shrikrishna (Krish) Singh of Auctus Publishers, whose passion for the written word has given urgent and important voices their choir. Thank you for choosing to share mine.

Tony Wood taught me, by his example, that art is worth pursuing. And Amity Wood allowed me to turn our lives into literature. Boundless appreciation.

Blessings to the friends that I love and the friends who love me, and all the women who listened.

To my parents, grandparents, aunts, uncles, brothers, sisters-in-law, nieces, nephews and cousins for giving me an origin in the world and a place to which I can return. As Bubbe Ida maintained, "We are rich in family."

www.ingramcontent.com/pod-product-compliance
Lightning Source LLC
Chambersburg PA
CBHW070949080526
44587CB00015B/2248